RYA ADVANCED SAILING

© RYA
Third Edition 2019
Reprinted December 2020
Reprinted March 2022
Reprinted March 2023
Reprinted July 2024
The Royal Yachting Association
RYA House, Ensign Way,
Hamble, Southampton,
Hampshire SO31 4YA

Tel: 02380 604 100

Web: www.rya.org.uk

We welcome feedback on our publications at publications@rya.org.uk

You can check content updates for RYA publications at
www.rya.org.uk/go/bookschangelog

ISBN 978-1-910017098
RYA Order Code G12

All rights reserved. No part of this publication may be reproduced,
stored in a retrieval system, or transmitted, in any form or by any means,
electronic, mechanical, photocopying, recording or otherwise, without
prior permission in writing from the publishers.
A CIP record of this book is available from the British Library

Note: While all reasonable care has been taken in the preparation of this
book, the publisher takes no responsibility for the use of the methods or
products or contracts described in this book.

Cover design: Pete Galvin
Illustrations: Pete Galvin
Photographic credits: James Eaves, Glide Free Design,
Provela, Waszp, Paul Wyeth
Typesetting and design: Velveo Design
Proofreading: Matthew Gale
Printed in the UK

CONTENTS

	INTRODUCTION	4
1	SEAMANSHIP SKILLS	5
2	DEALING WITH INVERSION CAPSIZES	32
3	DAY SAILING	37
4	SAILING WITH SPINNAKERS	66
5	TRAPEZING	86
6	START RACING	89
7	PERFORMANCE SAILING	105
8	THE RYA NATIONAL SAILING SCHEME	130
	GLOSSARY	131

INTRODUCTION

Dinghy sailing can bring enjoyment and a sense of challenge to you no matter your age or background – there is something for everyone. It's an amazing way to get out into the natural environment and enjoy all the outdoors has to offer.

This book has been created to support you on your journey through the RYA National Sailing Scheme and can be used as a reference guide throughout your time afloat.

One of the most appealing parts of sailing is the range of boats that you can use, and there is something to fit anyone from dinghies to multihulls, and keelboats. Throughout this book you will find certain techniques are generic across all boats, and others are more boat specific.

I hope you enjoy your time afloat as much as I do. Happy Sailing!

Liz McMaster
Chief Instructor, Dinghy, Wing & Windsurfing

Words in red have their definitions in the Glossary on pages 131–132.

1 SEAMANSHIP SKILLS

To carry out any of the manoeuvres in this section, it is good practice to follow these easy steps:

- PLAN: Take a moment to ensure that you, your crew and equipment are fully prepared. Think about what you are trying to achieve, and communicate.
- APPROACH: Approach so that the manoeuvre is as simple as possible. If you need to stop, what force will stop you? If you need to turn, what will help you turn?
- MANOEUVRE: Carry out the technique, smoothly and under control.
- ESCAPE: What actions shall I take if there is an unforeseen situation or a misjudgement?

Launching and Recovery

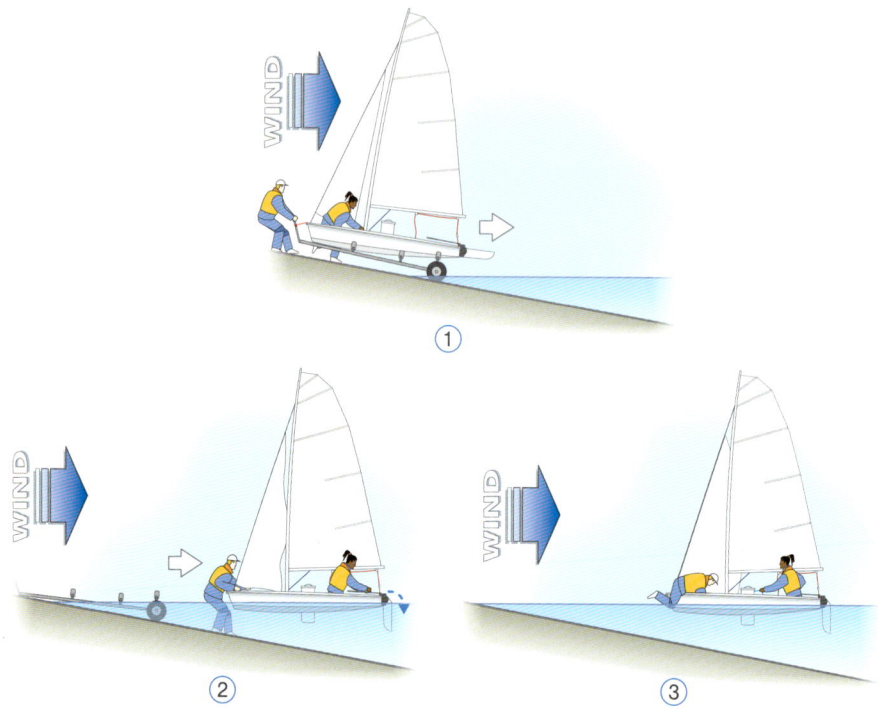

Launching from a Windward Shore (Wind Blows off the Shore)

- Rig the boat and hoist the sails ashore, furl the jib if possible, bow pointing into the wind. Attach the rudder if the blade can be held up.
- Ensure sheets run free and launch with the bow into the wind, stern first.
- The crew holds the boat in water deep enough for the helm to prepare the rudder. If your boat has a daggerboard, set it down far enough for the boom to clear the top of it.
- When the area to leeward is clear, the crew pushes the bow off and climbs in. The helm backs the jib to turn the bow away from the shore.
- The wind will take you away from the shore, making for a simple departure.
- Before fully sheeting sails in, set the rudder and centreboard.

TOP TIP
Ensure you stay on a training run to stop the accidental gybe.

Launching High-performance Boats

Fully battened sails are harder to depower, so to maintain control:

- Hoist sails ashore just before launching.
- Leave sail controls slack as the boat is launched (mainsheet, kicker, Cunningham).
- On return, once ashore, drop the mainsail immediately.

Dinghies with little inherent stability and fully battened sails will be easier to control afloat if the crew boards first, balancing the boat while setting the centreboard and jib. The helm pushes the boat off, climbing aboard over the stern or the side, with wind pressure on the sails providing stability.

Catamarans are sometimes better launched with the rudders and daggerboards (if fitted) raised, sails flapping and crew hanging on the bow to act as a sea anchor. The catamaran stays head to wind and drifts out before lowering rudders and sailing away.

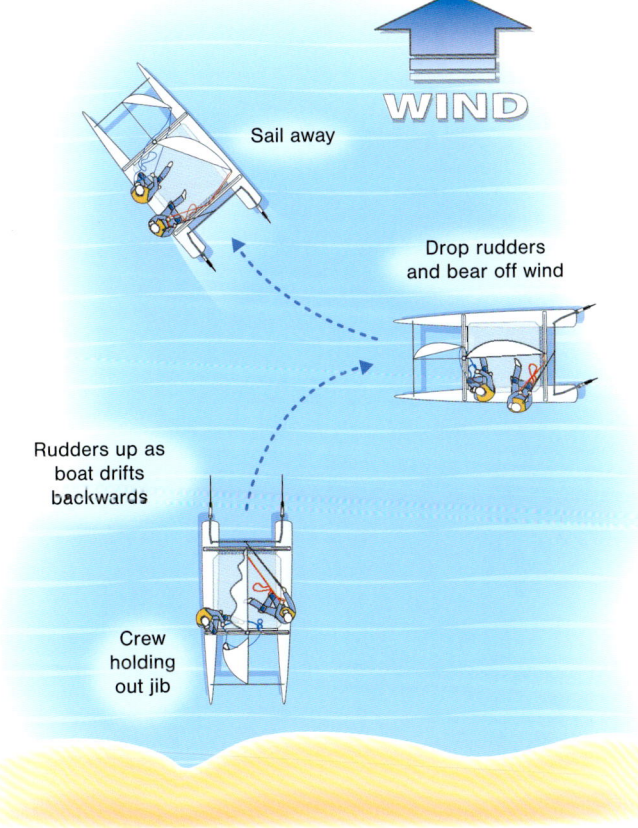

Returning to a Windward Shore

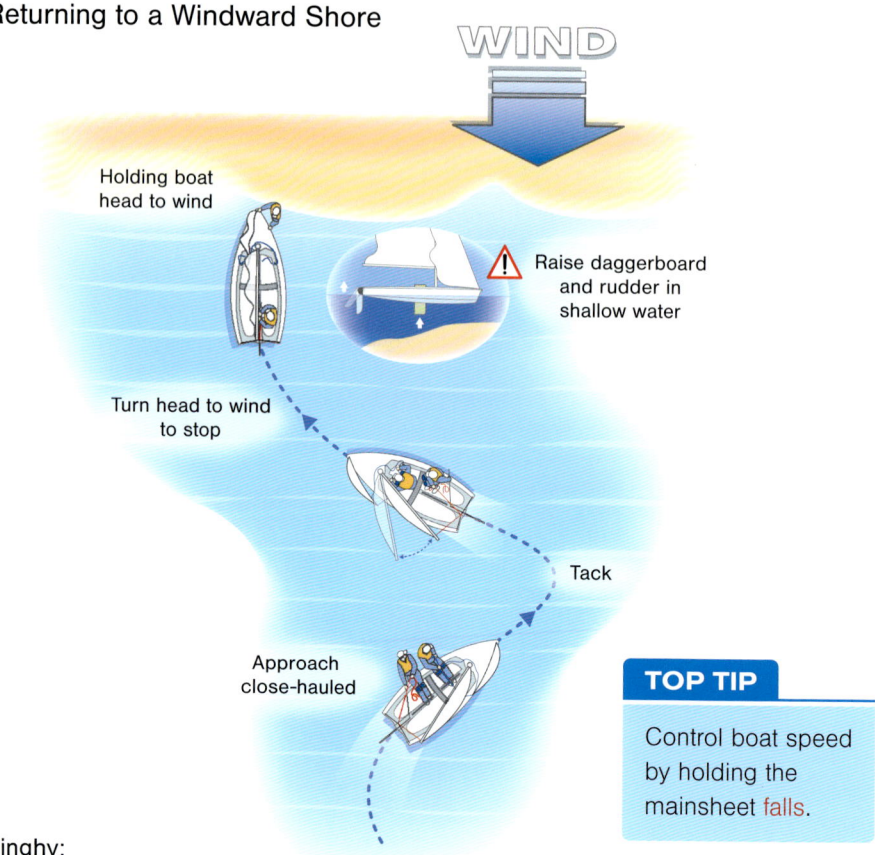

Dinghy:

Step 1:

- Sail toward the landing area on a close reach, taking account of the tidal flow and leeway as the board is raised.
- Raise the centreboard a little and release the rudder hold-down mechanism, partially raising the rudder if necessary.
- Let the jib fly or furl it.

Step 2:

- Sail slowly towards the shore with the mainsail partially flapping.
- Control the boat speed with the mainsheet. Ease fully as you reach the shore.

Step 3:

- Before the boat touches the shore the crew raises the centreboard and exits to windward to take hold of the bow. Make holding the boat easier by dropping the mainsail as soon as possible after landing.

Multihull:

Step 1:
- Sail toward the landing area on a close reach, taking account of the tidal flow and leeway.
- Raise the centreboard (if fitted) a little and raise the leeward rudder.
- Let the jib fly or furl it.
- Let off the mainsheet falls and play the traveller.

Step 2:
- Sail slowly towards the shore with the mainsail partially flapping (filling and spilling zone).
- Control the boat speed with the mainsheet traveller.
- Ease fully as you reach the shore. Remove the mainsheet block.

Step 3:
- Before the boat touches the shore the helm raises the rudders and the crew exits to windward or between the hulls to take hold of the boat.
- Make holding the boat easier by dropping the mainsail as soon as possible after landing.

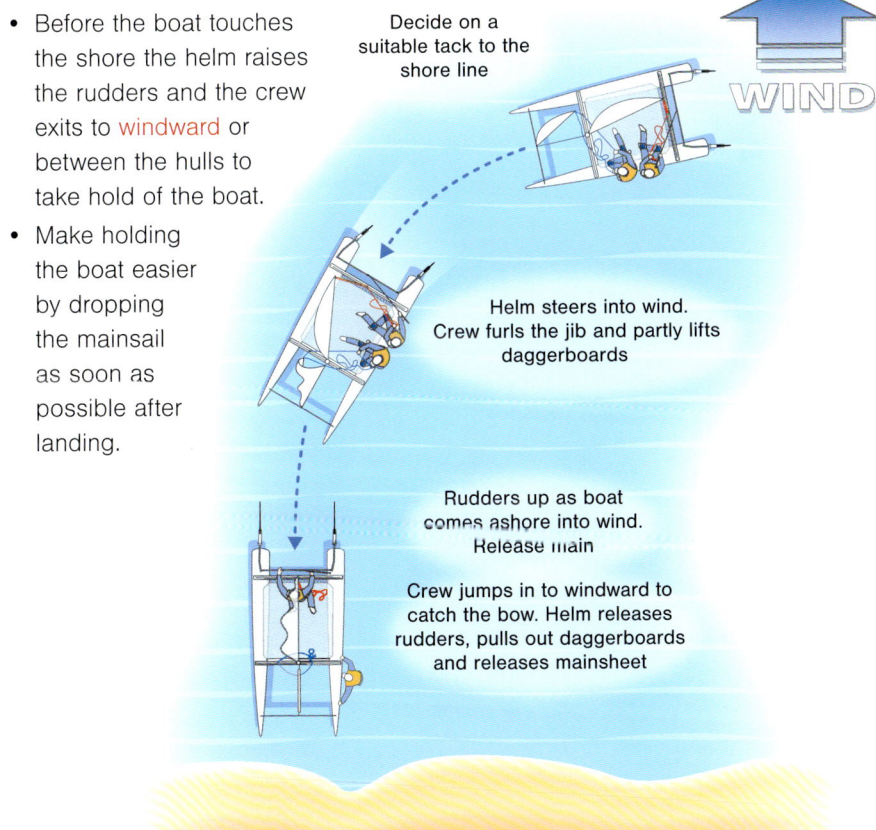

Decide on a suitable tack to the shore line

Helm steers into wind. Crew furls the jib and partly lifts daggerboards

Rudders up as boat comes ashore into wind. Release main

Crew jumps in to windward to catch the bow. Helm releases rudders, pulls out daggerboards and releases mainsheet

Launching from a Lee Shore (Wind onto the Shore)

With the wind blowing onto the shore there are additional considerations.

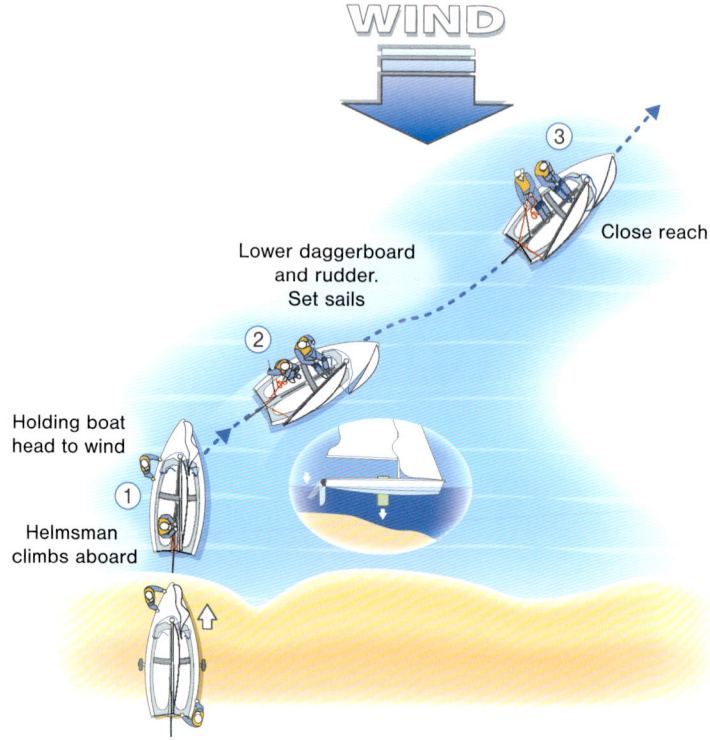

Dinghy:

- Hoist the jib on shore (furl if possible).
- Launch and turn the boat head to wind with the crew holding the boat in water deep enough to keep it from hitting the bottom.
- The helm can now hoist the main, either from shallow water beside the boat or aboard.
- As you hold the boat head to wind, note the angle relative to the shore. If the port side of the boat is nearer the shore, leave on port tack. If the starboard side is nearer, leave on starboard tack.
- With your preferred tack chosen, check the centreboard and rudder are down as far as possible, and that the sailing area is clear.
- The crew gives a firm push into deeper water and climbs in as the helm sets the rudder and sheets in the mainsail.
- The crew lowers the centreboard fully and sets the jib.

Bow-first Launching from a Lee Shore

Boats with fully battened sails and little inherent stability or those launching into waves will not be able to hoist sails afloat.

Dinghy:

- Hoist sails ashore and launch the boat bow first. This presents the 'V' section to the waves.
- Move the boat into deep water quickly so it does not drop off a wave onto the trolley. If the beach shelves gradually, carry the boat in. Ensure you have enough carriers to avoid a back injury.
- Depart using the same considerations for the preferred tack, with crew on board first.

Multihull:

- Hoist the jib on shore (furl if possible).
- Launch and turn the boat head to wind with the crew holding the boat in water deep enough to keep it from hitting the bottom. The helm can hoist the main.
- As the crew holds the boat head to wind, note the angle relative to the shore. If the port side of the boat is nearer the shore, leave on port tack. If the starboard side is nearer, leave on starboard tack.
- With your preferred tack chosen, check the rudder (on the deep-water side) is down as far as possible, and the sailing area is clear.
- The crew gives a firm push into deeper water and climbs in as the helm sets the windward rudder and sheets in the mainsail and plays the traveller.
- The crew sets the jib.

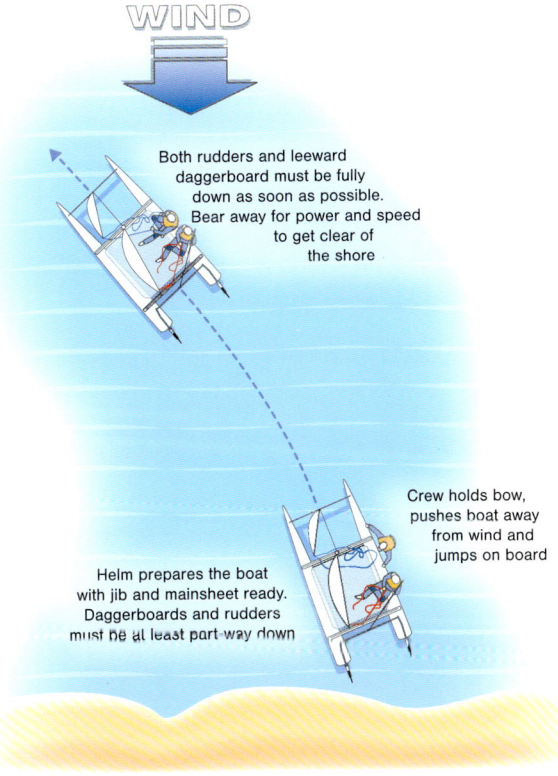

Both rudders and leeward daggerboard must be fully down as soon as possible. Bear away for power and speed to get clear of the shore

Crew holds bow, pushes boat away from wind and jumps on board

Helm prepares the boat with jib and mainsheet ready. Daggerboards and rudders must be at least part-way down

Returning to a Lee Shore

GOLDEN RULE

Make sure you can stop. With the wind astern, easing the sheets will not depower the sail. Reduce sail area to slow the boat.

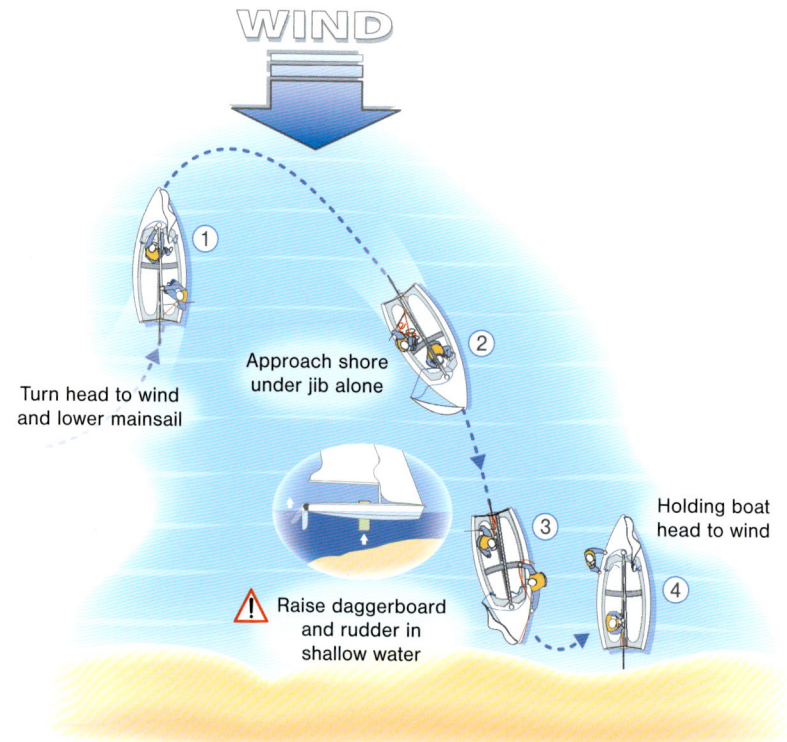

Dinghy:

Step 1:

- Select the best point to land while the crew checks the main halyard will run free. Consider streaming the halyard overboard.
- Sail uptide of the landing area.
- Turn head to wind, drop the main and raise the centreboard to one-third.

Step 2:
- Back the jib to turn the boat towards your chosen landing spot.
- As you approach the shore, lose speed by easing the jib sheet until the sail is flying free, or furl the jib.

Step 3:
- The crew jumps out and turns the boat into the wind by holding the painter (if fitted) as the helm raises or removes the rudder.
- If your boat has a forestay, consider dropping the jib.

Multihull:

Step 1:
- Select the best point to land while the crew checks the main halyard will run free. Consider streaming the halyard overboard.
- Sail uptide of the landing area.
- Turn head to wind, drop the main and raise the centreboards to one-third (if fitted).
- Consider raising the leeward rudder at this time.

Step 2:
- Back the jib to turn the boat towards your chosen landing spot.
- As you approach the shore, lose speed by easing the jib until the sail is flying free, or furl the jib.

Step 3:
- The crew jumps out and allows the boat to turn into the wind by holding the painter, shroud or crossbeam as the helm raises or removes the rudders.

Returning in waves requires co-ordinated help from a shore crew. Make sure you are aware of the system before sailing in and establish the signals to be used.

When the shore crew signal they are ready, begin your approach. To avoid surfing down a wave and burying the bow, follow the back of a wave in quickly, board raised and rudder released. Sail positively to the spot indicated and the shore crew will lift you and your boat clear before the arrival of the next wave.

TOP TIP

To keep the halyard tangle free so the sail can be swiftly lowered, flake the coiled halyard over the windward side prior to uncleating. It should trail behind the boat.

Picking up a Mooring

The principles for picking up a mooring or coming alongside a boat or jetty are the same.

Remember the key principles: Plan, Approach, Manoeuvre, Escape.

> **GOLDEN RULE**
>
> Make a steady and controlled approach, depowering the boat fully so you lie to the tide.

Wind and Tide Together

Dinghy/Keelboat/Multihull:

- Run a mooring line from the bow in preparation.
- Sail to a position downwind of, and away from, the buoy.
- Approach on a close reach, controlling power and speed (spill and fill zone) – a multihull plays the traveller.
- Aim to bring the buoy onto the windward side of the bow. If the boat is moving too fast, sail away and try again.
- Once at the buoy, raise the centreboard as the crew secures the boat to the buoy using a round turn and two half-hitches or a bowline.
- Drop and stow the sails (furl the jib).
- Raise (or remove) the rudder.

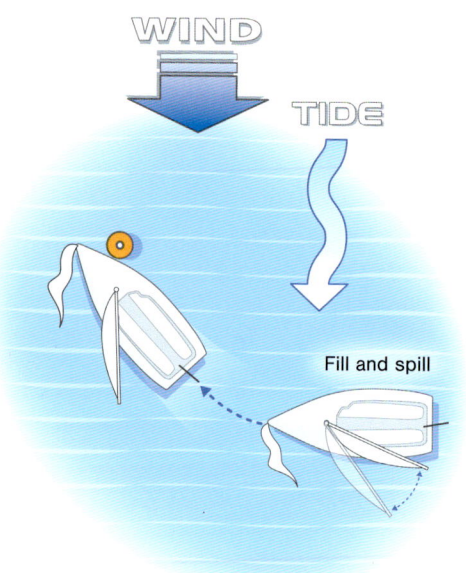

Fill and spill

When mooring a catamaran, attach a bridle line between both bows and the mooring to prevent the boat from swinging or fouling the mooring chain.

> **TOP TIP**
>
> To determine the tidal flow, look at the mooring buoys. The small grab buoy will lie downtide of the large mooring buoy. A stronger current increases the distance between the two.

Wind and Tide Opposed

- Position the boat upwind of the mooring buoy. Prepare to lower the mainsail.
- Turn head to wind and lower the mainsail. Back the jib to turn the boat downwind and raise the centreboard to one-third.
- Ease the jib (or furl) to slow the boat as you make the final approach, helm controlling the jib as the crew prepares to take hold of the buoy.
- Let the jib fly so the tide stops the boat at the buoy. The crew can now secure the boat.
- Raise (or remove) centreboard and rudder(s).

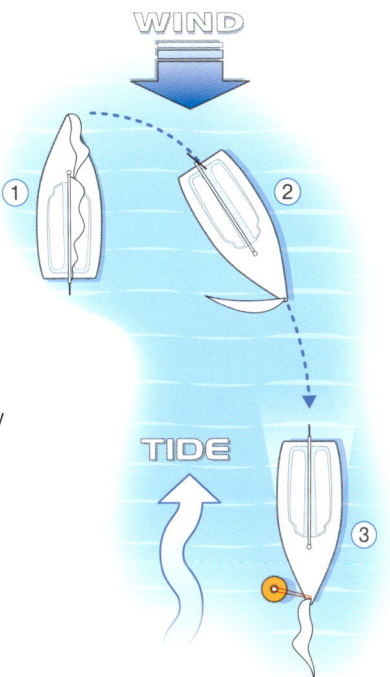

In light winds and a strong tide the jib might not have the power to carry you against the tide. In this situation, leave the mainsail up and approach from upwind. Lose speed by gradually lowering the main. Take care to sheet the main in a little to clear the shrouds (if fitted).

Leaving a Mooring

If the boat is pointing into the wind, attach (or lower) the rudder and hoist the sails while moored. Hoist the mainsail first to keep the boat pointing into the wind. Finally, hoist the jib, lower the board and slip the painter. Backing the jib will bring the bow away from the wind to put the boat on a reach. Sheet in and sail away. If the wind and tide are opposed, attach the rudder and hoist the jib, leaving it to fly (or furl). Slip the mooring line and sail away under jib alone to a clear area. Prepare the mainsail; turn the boat into the wind and hoist before bearing away to continue sailing. It may be easier to turn head to wind if the mainsail is partially raised before leaving.

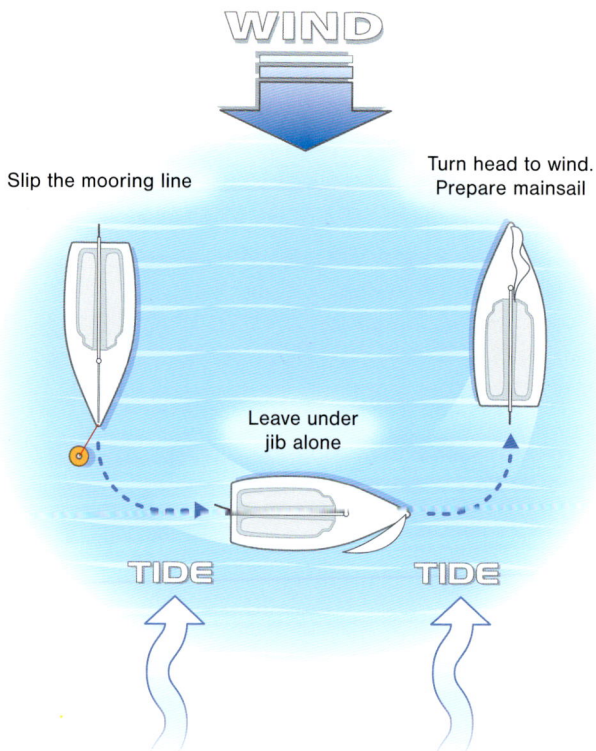

Coming alongside a Fixed Object or Boat

Make things easier by preparing first. Prepare mooring lines and deploy fenders if carried.

Wind and Tide Together

- Consider an escape route.
- Approach your destination on a close reach.
- Control speed using the mainsheet (or traveller), letting the jib flap (fill and spill zone).
- Ease the sheets as you turn the boat gently alongside.
- Raise the board as the crew secures the boat.
- Raise the rudders on multihull when secure.

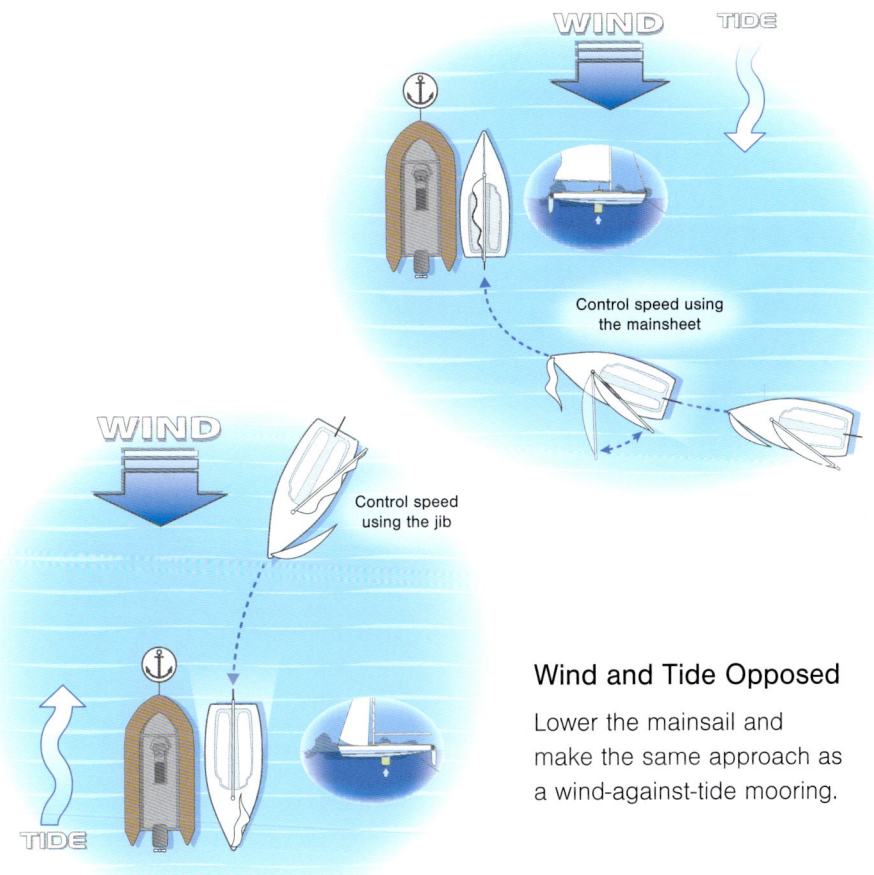

Wind and Tide Opposed

Lower the mainsail and make the same approach as a wind-against-tide mooring.

RYA Advanced Sailing

Wind across Tide

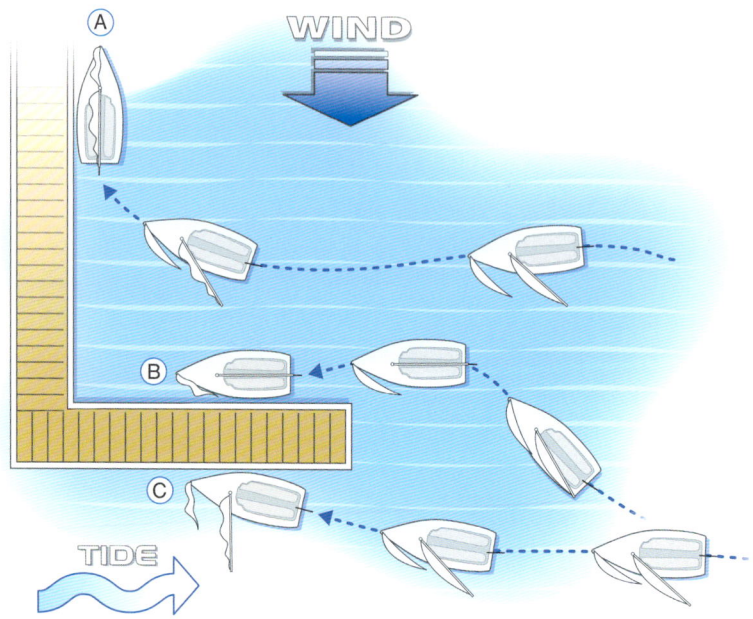

With wind direction across the flow of the tide:

- With the landing area at right angles to the tide, slowly approach into the tide on a close reach. Turn into the wind to bring you to the downtide side of the landing (A).
- With the landing area parallel to the tide, approach on a close reach into the tide. If landing on the windward side, drop the mainsail and approach into the tide under jib alone (B). If landing on the leeward side, ease sails fully to stop alongside (C).

GOLDEN RULE

Although similar to mooring, there is a risk of collision; always plan an escape route.

Anchoring

Some sailing dinghies and catamarans do not carry anchors, as the boats would not lie to an anchor in a stable position. However, some keelboats and day-sailing dinghy sailors would consider an anchor absolutely essential.

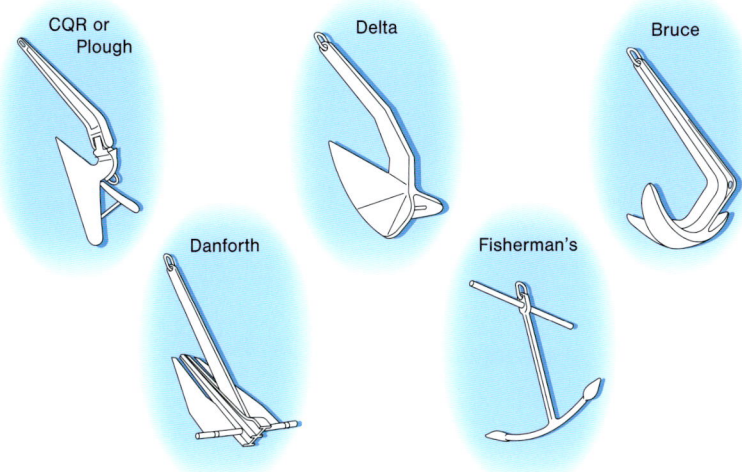

Remember to tie the anchor down when not in use (keep it in a bucket or stow it). Select an appropriate anchorage, taking into consideration important factors such as depth of water and your boat's draft, tide state, sufficient anchor warp, and the seabed. If necessary, use a chart and tide table to obtain information regarding the nature of the seabed, obstructions, and the depth of water.

The 'Day Sailing' chapter will provide you with some useful information on tidal flow. See pages 47–50 for more details.

RYA Advanced Sailing 19

Approach: Wind and Tide Together

- Approach the chosen site on a close reach, using the mainsheet (or traveller) to control the speed.
- Furl or lower the jib if possible or let it fly. Release the mainsheet to bring the boat to a stop.
- Lower the anchor over the windward side of the boat and raise the centreboard (the rudders on a multihull).
- The mainsail will hold the boat's position relative to the wind as you drift back.
- Make sure the anchor is holding. Check that two in-line objects on the land do not change position in relation to each other. This is known as 'taking a transit'.
- When the anchor is holding, lower the mainsail.
- If the anchor is not holding, let out more warp. If this fails, retrieve the anchor and make another attempt.

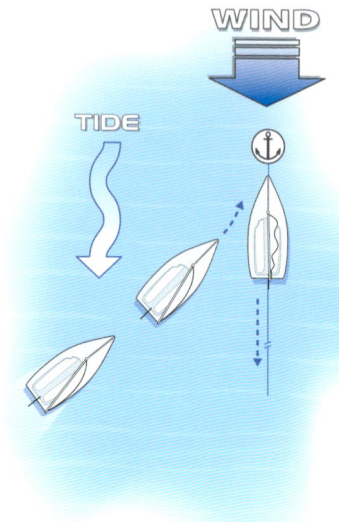

Before you start, prepare the anchor, ensuring it is attached to a strongpoint on the boat and will run freely from the bow. A short length of chain makes the anchor more effective. Line and chain should be at least three times the depth of water. The anchor line is known as a warp.

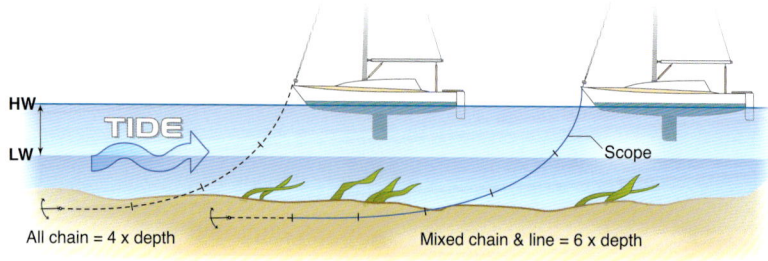

All chain = 4 x depth   Mixed chain & line = 6 x depth

TOP TIP

If you do not have a bow fairlead, run the anchor line through a small rope loop tied through a bow fitting. Looping around the forestay can snap it.

Approach: Wind and Tide Opposed

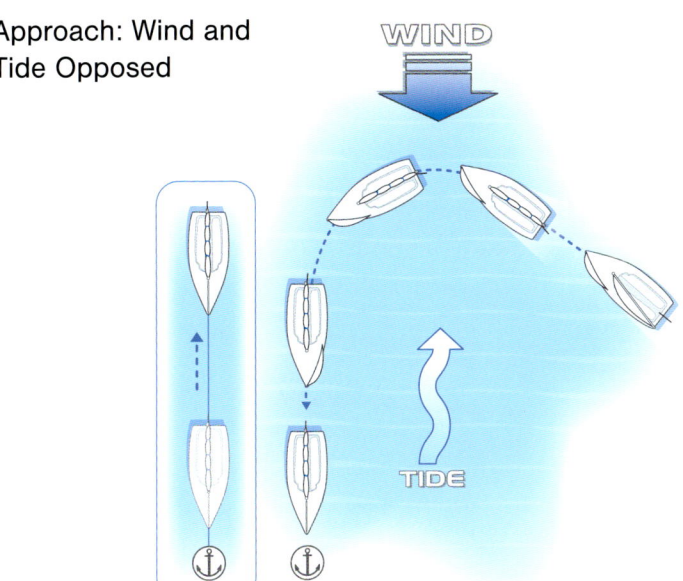

- Anchor the boat into the tide, with the boat pointing downwind and the mainsail lowered.
- Go head to wind upwind of your chosen spot and lower the mainsail.
- Make the same approach as a wind-against-tide mooring.
- When the boat is stopped in the correct place, lower the anchor and let the warp out as the boat drifts back in the tide.
- Check the anchor is holding using a transit.

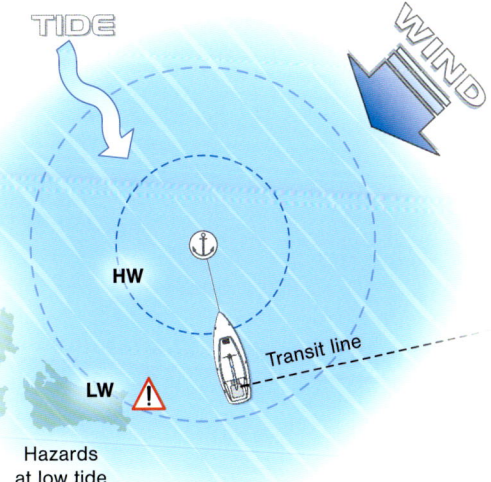

Leaving your Anchorage

Leave using the same method as leaving a mooring, bringing the anchor on board rather than letting a mooring line go. Take care to bring it under the jib sheets to avoid tangles.

> **GOLDEN RULE**
>
> Drop the anchor uptide of where you want the boat to lie and allow room to swing if the tide turns.

Heaving to

Heaving to is used whenever you wish to depower the boat and hold it at a constant angle to the wind while floating free. This is a more stable position than simply lying to with both sails flapping, due to the jib being aback.

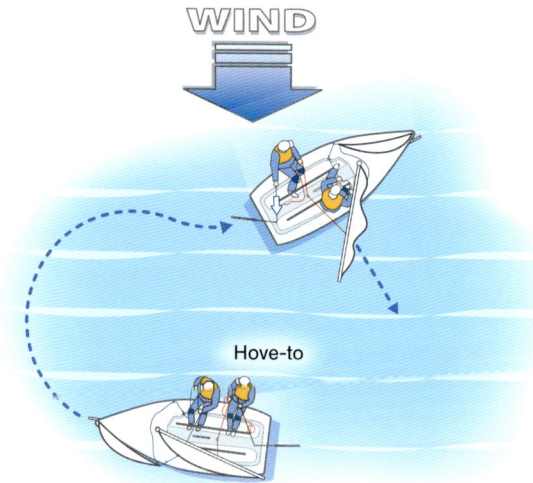

Hove-to

- The easiest method to heave to is to tack, leaving the jib cleated on the old side.
- Select a point with clear water downwind or downtide, whichever is the stronger.
- Cleat the jib aback with the mainsheet fully eased.
- Hold the tiller to leeward, and raise the centreboard halfway.
- Maintain a good lookout and be aware of leeway.

Reefing Afloat in Strong Winds

As the wind becomes stronger you may need to reduce sail area. Methods vary, as different classes use a variety of reefing systems. Make things easier by reefing ashore, at a mooring or at anchor. If none of these are viable, sail into clear water and heave to, preferably on starboard.

Slab Reefing

A slab-reefing system includes a rope fed from the boom through an eye in the leech of the sail. A second eye is situated at the luff, above the downhaul/Cunningham.

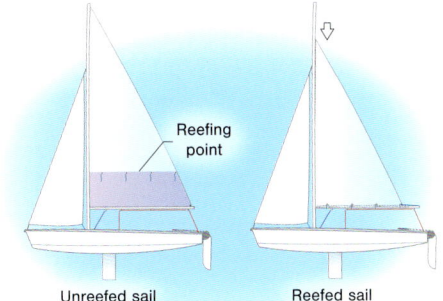

Unreefed sail   Reefed sail

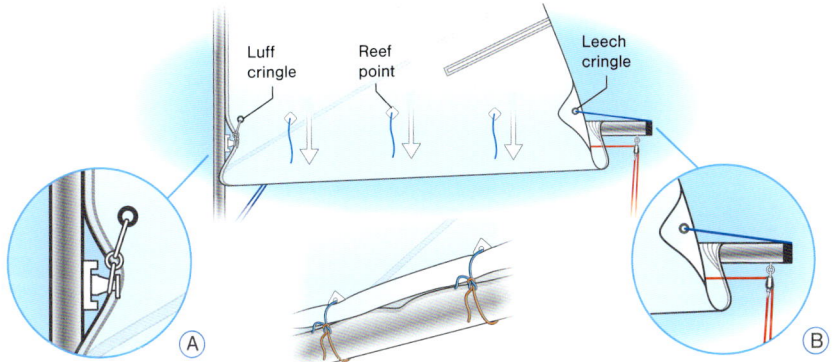

- To reef, partially lower the mainsail and feed the Cunningham through a higher eye in the luff.
- Pull tight (A).
- Pull the rope from the leech point to bring the eye down to the boom (B). With some systems you can do this first without lowering the sail. Ensure the kicker (vang) is loosened.
- Many systems include elastic along the sail or boom to hold the excess sail area neatly.
- Many systems include a second or third rope and eyelets above the first to take further reefs.
- Slab reefing on a multihull usually has a bungee to stow excess sail at the bottom.

Round the Boom (Aft Mainsheet)

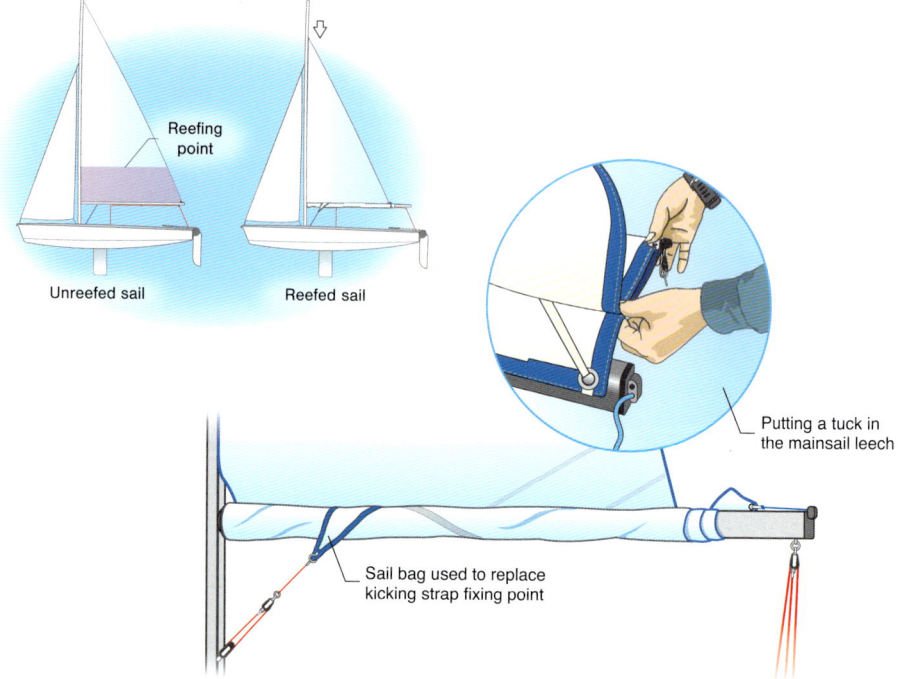

Putting a tuck in the mainsail leech

Sail bag used to replace kicking strap fixing point

Dinghy and Keelboat:
- Ensure the main halyard is streaming.
- Lower the mainsail about halfway.
- Remove the kicking strap and mainsheet block from the boom and the lower batten from the sail.
- Tuck about 50cm of the leech down to the boom and roll with a reefing strop or sail bag to take the place of the kicking strap fixing point.
- Re-attach the mainsheet and place the boom back on the gooseneck.
- Hoist the sail, attach the kicking strap (to reefing strop or sail bag) and sail away.
- A good tip is to pull down on the back of the boom to tighten the reefing rolls.

Multihull:
- Ensure the main halyard is streaming.
- Lower the mainsail about halfway.
- Remove the downhaul and mainsheet block from the boom and lower the mainsail.

- Troll the mainsail from the bottom and secure using the bungee (Dart 16 and other multihulls).
- Re-attach the mainsheet block to the new cringle and place the boom back on the gooseneck if fitted.
- Hoist the mainsail, attach the downhaul and sail away.

> **TOP TIP**
>
> Use a smaller jib with a reefed mainsail or reduce the jib using the roller mechanism.

Round the Mast

Most single-handed dinghies furl the sail around the mast to reef, or use a smaller mast and sail. With the sail flapping, remove the kicker from the mast and uncleat the clew outhaul. Rotate the base of the mast to furl the sail and then simply re-attach the kicker and cleat the outhaul.

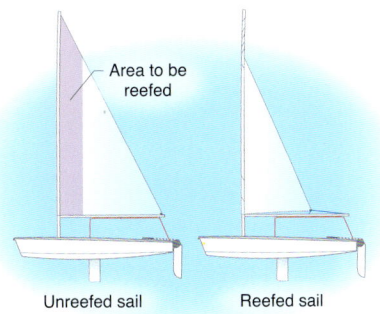

Area to be reefed

Unreefed sail   Reefed sail

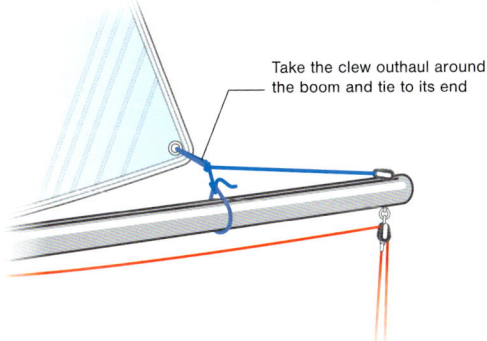

Take the clew outhaul around the boom and tie to its end

Fully Battened Sails

When sailing in strong winds, depower the sail by pulling the Cunningham/downhaul on fully, adding lots of kicking strap to bend the mast and some outhaul to flatten the lower part of the sail. The most common mistake is to sail with too much power due to insufficient Cunningham/downhaul and kicker. Only a few fully battened sails will reef, such as on the Dart 16.

A reefed catamaran sail is often flat and underpowered, so be careful not to oversheet when sailing.

Man Overboard (MOB)

Although it does not happen often, people can and do fall overboard when sailing. In some two-person dinghies the boat may capsize after you lose someone over the side. With more stable boats you can sail back and recover your crew. Both the MOB and boat are equally influenced by the tidal flow, so this does not need to be considered.

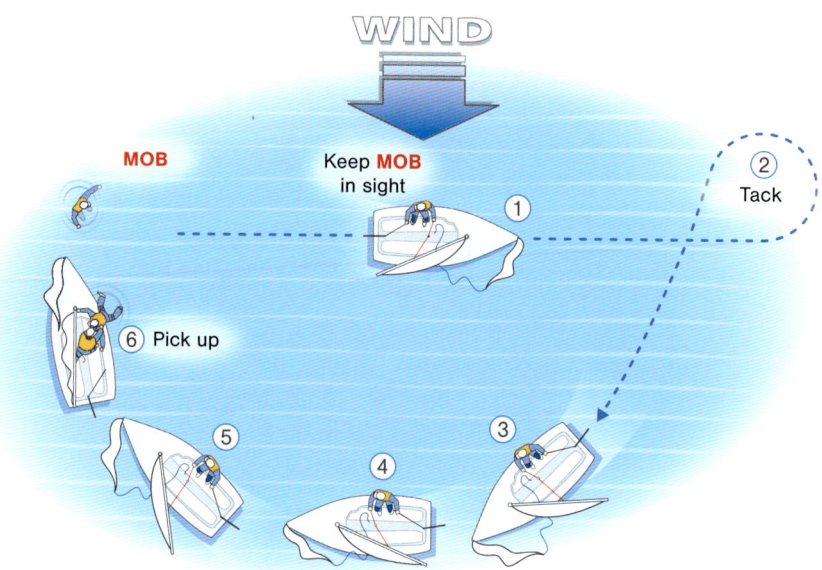

Step 1:
As soon as the person falls overboard, regain control of the boat, check they are okay and signal your intention to return. Keep an eye on them at all times. Turn onto a reach, sailed correctly when the boom is held a few inches off the shrouds, and the sail still has some (not full) power.

Step 2:
Leave the jib flapping and prepare to tack, allowing yourself plenty of room to slow the boat as you return. Tack and bear away onto a broad reach or reach.

Step 3:
Sail until you can approach on a close reach. The flapping jib is a useful indicator of wind position.

Step 4:
Once approaching on a close reach, depower the main to control your boat speed (fill and spill zone). Stop with the MOB by the windward shroud. If the boat is still moving, twitch the tiller to windward to prevent the boat tacking on top of the MOB.

Step 5:
Bring the MOB aboard over the side or through the open transom, taking care to keep the boat across the wind as you do so.

On the final approach, if you are sailing too fast or you drift away from the person, sail away and complete the technique on the other tack.

TOP TIP

If you are uncertain when to head up, point the boat towards the MOB. If the sail flaps to leeward you are in the right place. If still powered up, bear away and try again. If you find you are head to wind, sail past and tack round to try again on the opposite tack.

Catamarans

Take great care not to capsize the catamaran after someone has fallen overboard. Follow the steps above, but gybe the catamaran and on the approach collect the person between the hulls by the cross beam.

GOLDEN RULE

Keep an eye on the person in the water throughout the manoeuvre.

Boats with Racks or Wings

If your boat has racks, most techniques remain the same. It is often easier to reboard the boat through the transom. Extra consideration is required when coming alongside. If coming alongside an inflatable safety boat, rest the rack on the tubes for stability.

TOP TIP

If your boat has racks and you are alongside an inflatable, ask the crew to sit on the rack and tube, locking the two boats together.

Ropework

Whipping the End of a Rope

Many modern ropes can be heat-sealed at the ends. If not, whipping twine can be used to prevent fraying.

1. Lay a loop along the rope.
2. Wind 10–20 turns over the loop very tightly.
3. Finish by threading the end through the loop and drawing it under the windings.

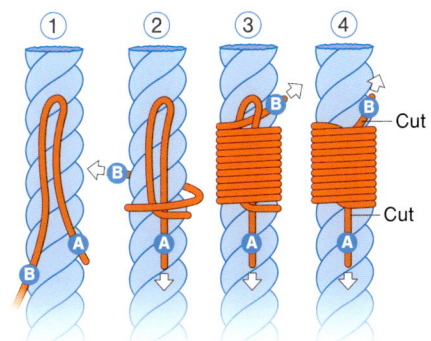

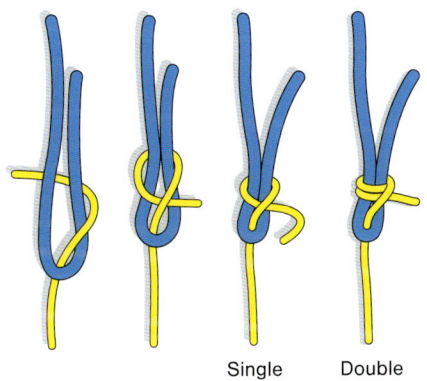

Single   Double

Sheet Bend

- This knot will join two lines of unequal thickness.
- The double sheet bend is a more secure version.

Fisherman's Bend

A good alternative to a bowline for attaching to a ring. The first half-hitch is trapped under the round turn.

Sailing without a Rudder

This exercise introduces important principles of boat control and may be useful if you have a broken rudder. It provides a fantastic way of understanding the forces on a boat.

The boat is steered by altering the balance and sail setting. Practise in a clear area with a steady and light wind. This manoeuvre is not possible in catamarans.

- Sheet the mainsail in to luff up.
- Sheet the jib in to bear away.
- Heel to leeward to luff up.
- Heel to windward to bear away.

Before you start: Either raise the rudder on the uphaul or immobilise the rudder by very loosely securing it to the centreline of the boat with a strong piece of elastic. This will allow you to regain control again quickly if necessary. Try this in light winds to start with, on a quiet and safe piece of water, in a dinghy with a jib (with or without a crew).

- Raise the board by one-third.
- Reef the mainsail if necessary.
- Consider reducing the number of falls in the mainsheet.
- To avoid over-steering, practise by setting the jib, controlling the mainsail and balancing yourself. Learn to work with the crew later.
- Set the jib, set the weight (crew) and play the main.
- Keep movements small when moving weight as this is a key to having success. The main aim is to keep the boat flat to keep it going straight.

Firstly, it is important to understand how the boat behaves if it is heeled towards or away from the wind

Secondly, learn what happens if you sheet in the jib and ease the mainsail, and vice versa.

By heeling the boat to leeward and/or sheeting in the mainsail you can turn the boat into the wind. Similarly, by heeling the boat on top of yourself and/or sheeting in the jib you can make the boat bear away.

TOP TIP

When sailing without using the rudder, raise the centreboard by one-third. This reduces the heeling and turning forces by raising the centre of lateral resistance and moving it back.

Sailing without a Centreboard

If the centreboard is lost or damaged you will need to use other methods to help the boat point to windward and minimise leeway. The easiest way is to move your weight as far forwards to the bow as possible, sinking the 'V' section down to act as an improvised board. The boat will not point as high and will make greater leeway, but some progress to windward is possible using this technique. You can heel the boat slightly to leeward which will help drive the board towards the wind. Consideration must also be given when tacking due to having a reduced pivot point – you can keep the jib on its original side for longer to help bring the bow through the wind.

Sailing Backwards

Sailing backwards can be really useful when leaving a crowded windward shore.

- Stop the boat directly head to wind. The centreboard should be half down, jib flapping.
- Crew sits forward of the boom, facing aft, and pulls the boom against the shroud, backing the mainsail. The sail will try to turn the stern away from the side it is on and drive the boat backwards.
- Helm sits, moving weight as far forward as possible, and counters the turn with a little rudder, tiller pushed away from the boom.
- Both helm and crew keep their weight towards the bow to lift the transom and remain sat down.
- Helm steers boat by pointing rudder in the direction of travel using small movements.
- To stop, push the tiller towards the boom. This will turn the boat away from you. When the boat has turned, sheet in the main and jib.
- Straighten the tiller as the boat sails away.

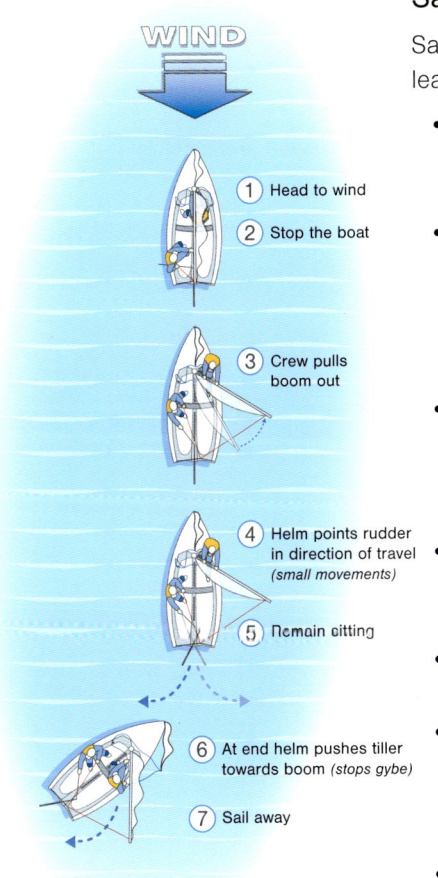

WIND

1. Head to wind
2. Stop the boat
3. Crew pulls boom out
4. Helm points rudder in direction of travel *(small movements)*
5. Remain sitting
6. At end helm pushes tiller towards boom *(stops gybe)*
7. Sail away

2 DEALING WITH INVERSION CAPSIZES

The best advice for dealing with inversions is: try not to let it happen! If you do get to the stage where you know the boat is going to capsize, try to step over and onto the centreboard to avoid the capsize altogether.

However, an inverted capsize should be a straightforward problem, provided the crew is aware of the risk of entanglement as the mast and rigging sinks. Most modern boats have self-draining cockpits and will probably have a limited air pocket once inverted. While more traditional designs will probably retain an air void once inverted they are likely to require bailing once righted.

In the illustration opposite, the crew has moved to the stern in order to remain clear if the boat inverts. The crew is in a safe position to watch the helm onto the centreboard, where she can stabilise the boat on its side.

If the boat does invert, both crew and helm move to the windward side and lean back on the centreboard, using a jib sheet (or righting line) to assist if necessary. Once the centreboard is within reach the heavier person should climb onto it and bring the mast horizontal, pointing downwind.

Once the boat is stable in a horizontal position, the lighter person goes into the boat via the stern to recover the spinnaker and release the kicker and mainsheet. Free the spinnaker halyard and carefully pull the downhaul to lower the spinnaker into the chute. If your boat has bags instead of a chute, gather the spinnaker using the upper sheet and one side of the sail, stowing it in the upper bag.

GOLDEN RULE

Safety first. Stay in contact with the boat but take care if the boat is inverting.

Note that, while this procedure will reduce the risk of the boat inverting on top of a crew member, some boats are more prone to inversion than others. Be aware of the risk of re-inversion at all times. One or two designs may even invert with someone fully on the centreboard.

Once the boat is ready, lean back to bring the boat up, scooping the crew aboard if possible.

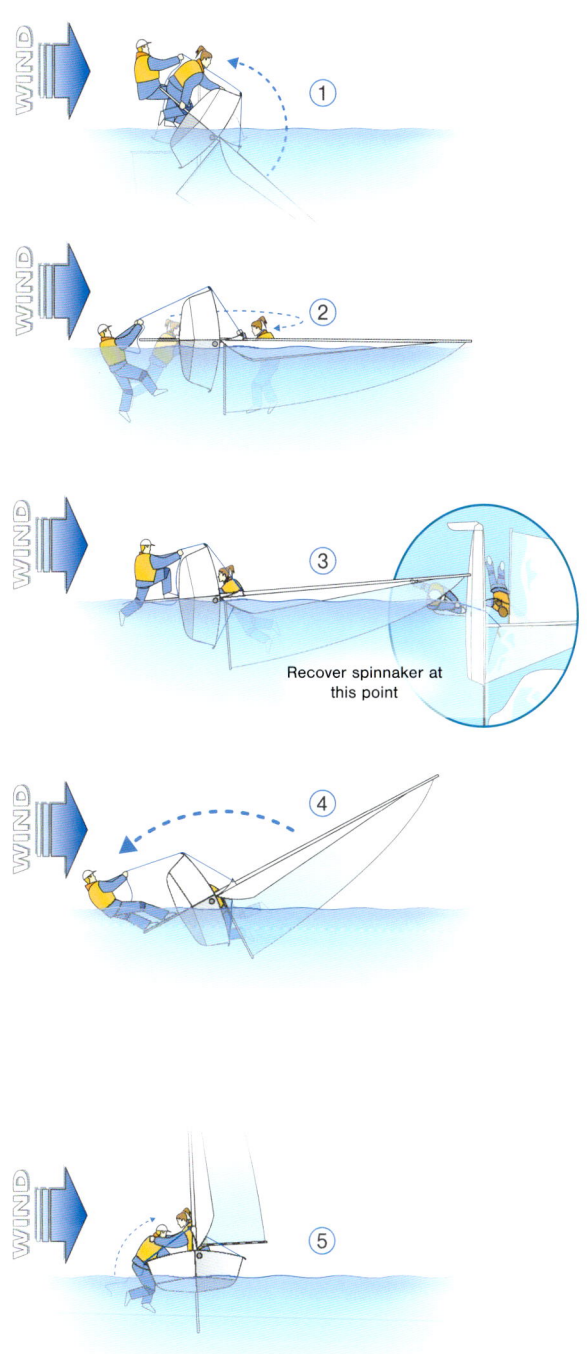

One very common problem is that the hull blows downwind of the rig. If the boat is righted from this position, the force on the sail is likely to capsize the boat on top of the unfortunate person who was on the centreboard. To avoid the problem, ask the crew to hang on to the toe straps to prevent the boat coming upright. Pull just the head of the sail out of the water so that the wind will spin it around to the leeward side. Then right the boat as normal. It is often easier to re-enter the boat over the transom. Once aboard, control the boat, grab the tiller, check the ropes and rudder and prepare to sail off.

> **GOLDEN RULE**
>
> Always lower the spinnaker at least partially into the chute/bags before bringing the boat up. You must fully or partially recover the spinnaker or you will almost certainly lose control of the righted boat or damage the spinnaker.

Multihull Capsizes

A full inversion can be solved by moving both crew and helm to the back of the leeward hull. The stern should sink, screwing the bows up. Use the righting line to pull the masthead to the surface.

Once the masthead is on the surface, move forward to the bows so that wind pressure on the trampoline swings the mast into the wind. Ensure you take the tension off the mainsheet block prior to righting. This depowers the mainsail. This makes righting the boat easier as the wind lifts the sail. Remember to hold on to the cross beams or lines underneath to stop the boat recapsizing.

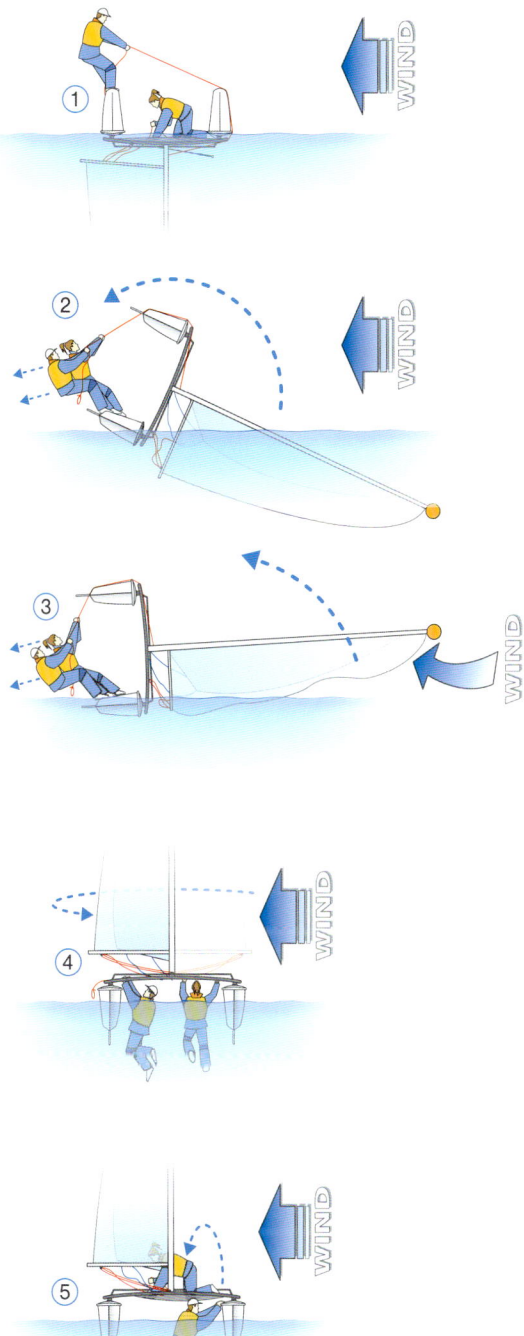

High-performance Safety

Modern dinghies are easy to sail very fast. Think ahead, leave plenty of room for manoeuvres and keep a good lookout, particularly under spinnaker.

If you do capsize, be aware of the risk of entanglement in standing or running rigging, or even the tiller extension. Trapeze hooks do occasionally foul on parts of the rigging, which can lead to an alarming or dangerous incident. To reduce the risk:

- Keep rope lengths to a minimum to avoid tangles.
- Re-tension or replace tensioning elastic regularly. Ensure there are no slack wires or string as they are a potential hazard.
- Carry a really sharp knife with a serrated edge.
- Always sail under control.
- Always tidy up loose sheet falls.
- Consider a breakaway trapeze hook.

One of the worst things that can happen is for the crew to become entangled as the boat inverts. It is much better to avoid this problem than to solve it. Consider how you would deal with entanglements on your particular boat. Know your boat. Under what circumstances will it invert? How quickly? Is there an air gap?

During training, you will often see masthead flotation being used. This can reduce the likelihood of inversion, and it's also used outside of high-performance sailing. However, if you are looking to race or train away from this environment, it is essential you learn to deal with inversions in safe surroundings. Always practise a full inversion without masthead flotation prior to a regatta.

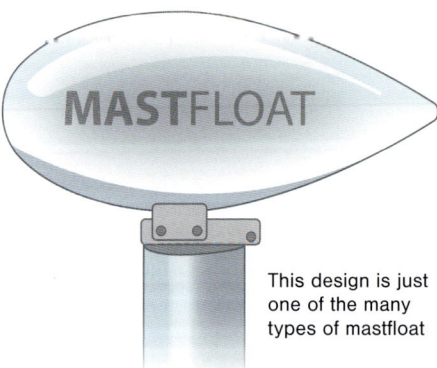

This design is just one of the many types of mastfloat

3 DAY SAILING

Small-boat day sailing is an enjoyable, fascinating and relaxing pastime, whether your horizon is the far end of the reservoir or further afield. Day sailing is a very safe activity providing you follow a few simple principles and plan your day to make the best use of the sailing area and conditions.

Equipment

Safety

The safety equipment you should carry will depend on the type of boat, the length and nature of the trip, the venue, and who is on board. Carry more rather than less, but not at the expense of weighing down the boat with things you are unlikely to use.

Water/Snacks
Spare clothes
Hat
Sun cream
Survival blanket
First aid kit
Small toolkit/Spares
Knife/Whistle
Waterproof wallet/Money
Means of communication

Changeable weather and capsizing are the most common issues when sailing in the UK, so always wear a buoyancy aid or lifejacket (whichever is most relevant to the craft you are sailing) and carry waterproofs and extra clothing. Always get an up-to-date, local, marine weather forecast.

If you are sailing in an area with few other boats, consider taking some means of communication in case of difficulty. Handheld VHFs or mobile phones (in a waterproof case) are useful, depending on location. The RYA Day Sailing course will teach you all you need to know about going on a short journey. Once you have gained more experience, you can start to plan your own day sail.

For safety, you should consider carrying flares (which should be stored dry), depending on the waters you decide to journey on. Flares have a limited shelf life, so always replace them before the expiry date. Day/night flares are useful to signal your position when in sight of rescue, while parachute flares are more effective in attracting attention from a distance. Always know how to launch your flares. Read the label and ensure they are in date.

Boat Choice

Choosing a stable and sensible dinghy or keelboat is essential. Many day-sailing sailors pay scant attention to rig tuning, but getting the mast position and rake right can make a huge difference to pointing ability and reducing the power – the difference between catching the tide and being several hours late. See Performance Sailing (chapter 7) for more information on tuning your rig.

Trailing

If you have your own boat and wish to trail to a different venue then you should consult and comply with the local regulations regarding towing, and load your dinghy sensibly. Further information on towing can be sought on the Highways Agency website.

Pre-planning

Before considering undertaking a short tidal or non-tidal passage it is necessary to do some basic pre-planning. We want the passage to be safe, enjoyable and free from unexpected hazards, so an outline plan of what you want to achieve, where you want to go and what to take with you should be considered. The number-one consideration should always be safety.

Equipment

Once we have made the decision to go on a short passage, before going near the water we need to consider what equipment we will need, both in the planning stages and also during the trip. A potential list could include:

- A chart plotter (this could be a smart phone running some software for navigation).
- An almanac or some method of accessing websites to identify local hazards, bylaws, call signs etc., in our proposed sailing area.
- Tide tables, or a smartphone app to get tidal information.
- Plotting instrumentation – including pencils, erasers, plotter, dividers, *Symbols and Abbreviations used on Admiralty Charts* (5011) if using an Admiralty Chart. Some charts have the symbols listed on the reverse.
- A chart of the proposed sailing area. Ensure it is in date or corrected accordingly.

Other considerations that should be taken into account before starting to form a detailed plan are:

- Tide will dictate where we go. Tidal interpretation is predictable because of history; therefore, it is a certainty in our plan.
- We should also consider the speed and leeway of our dinghy when planning, so we have an idea of Speed over the Ground (SOG) and Course over the Ground (COG), i.e. how much will the dinghy slip sideways when beating and in rough conditions, and what speed can we achieve, upwind and downwind?
- What are the local weather trends in our proposed area? Are they seasonal and will they affect our trip? What is the wind direction? What is the weather outlook?
- Other factors specific to the area like headlands, effects of sea and land breezes, any local tidal conditions, any major shipping movements in the area, buoyage, commercial traffic, local bylaws. The almanac will provide all this information.

Most if not all of the above information can be found in the equipment mentioned earlier, or from the internet.

Detailed Passage Planning

The primary consideration when starting to plan is the tide, if your trip is on tidal waters. If your trip is on non-tidal waters then you should consider weather, any local wind conditions, and where you are authorised to sail.

We can find most of this detail from an almanac, which is a great source of information, from the internet, and from various apps for smartphones. Whichever method you use it must be accurate and you need to ensure the proposed date and time of the journey follows the flow of the tide, where possible.

Once you have considered the tidal flow and decided on your date you can look at the details of the passage, taking into consideration all the other elements, SOG, COG, and most importantly a safety system. Think about safe havens, VHF or local telephone numbers for assistance, and hazards, just in case you get into difficulty from any unexpected gear failure or changes in the weather conditions.

Now we have all this information we can get to the actual passage planning.

Pilotage

You will need to find your way around while afloat. This is called pilotage. Small-boat pilotage only requires simple equipment and will very much depend on location. It is easy to become disorientated, even in moderate visibility, so always carry a chart and compass on coastal trips. Charts have a nasty habit of blowing away, so a waterproof notebook with a summary of the trip may be more practical. However, you may wish to carry a cut-out chart (which is waterproofed) of the immediate area for backup. The RYA Essential Navigation and Seamanship course is fantastic for furthering your knowledge in this area.

Interpreting Charts

Once you know a coastal area well, a very simple plan with a detailed weather forecast is often all that is required. In less familiar or complicated sailing areas, it pays to plan in more depth in advance.

Charts are a representation of the curved surface of the Earth on a flat sheet of paper. As a result, they are drawn using a system of latitude and longitude as a grid reference and scale. Distance is always measured in degrees, minutes and seconds of latitude on a scale up the side of the chart.

One minute of latitude is equal to one nautical mile (1 nautical mile = 1.12 statute miles). The vertical lines on the chart all relate to true north. Like land maps, charts use symbols to show useful and important features and hazards. Here, a bird's eye view of Namley Harbour shows how the chart relates to the coastline.

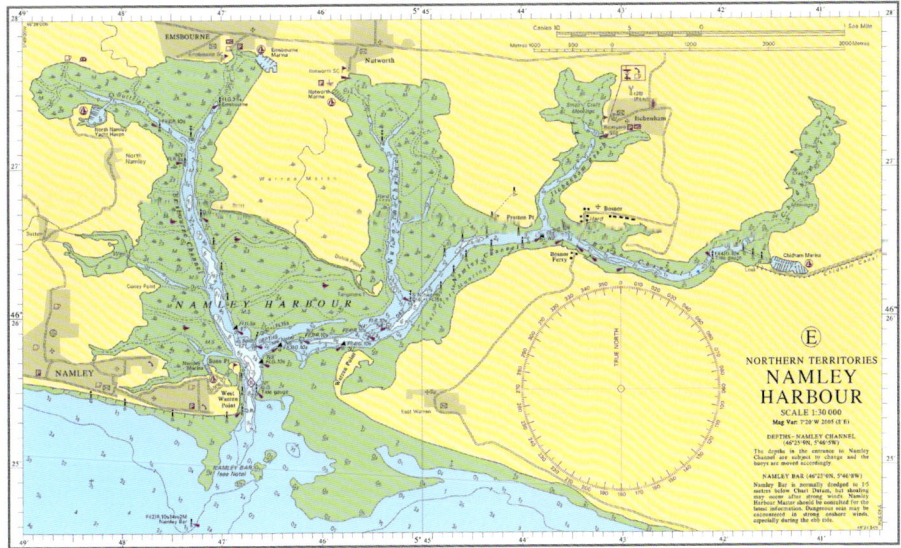

Symbols and Abbreviations used on Admiralty Charts (5011), published by the UK Hydrographic Office, can be used to identify features and symbols on the chart. On some charts the symbols are printed on the reverse, so a separate publication is not required.

The depth of water shown is 'lowest astronomical tide' – known as chart datum.

The black line along the coast represents the highest water level, i.e. the edge of the land. Depths which are underlined are drying heights, so they will dry out at low water. Be careful!

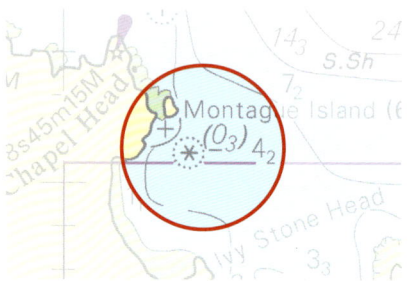

Direction is indicated in degrees by the compass rose printed on the chart. The compass points to magnetic north, which changes a tiny amount each year – not significant for basic pilotage. The difference between north on the chart and magnetic north is known as variation and is marked on the chart's compass rose.

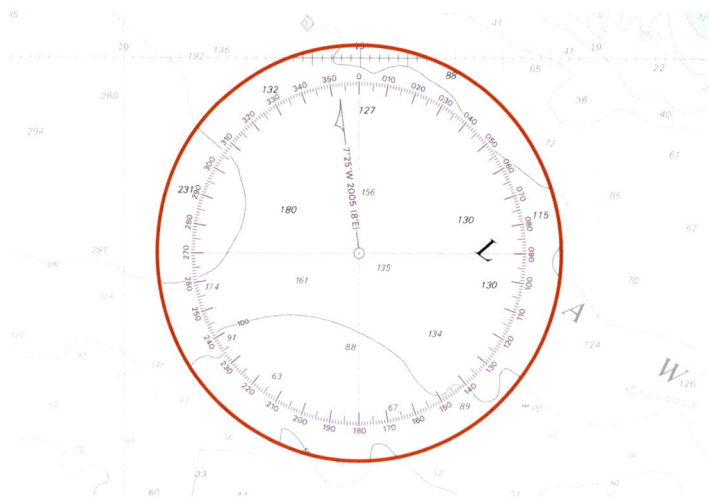

Weather Conditions

You do not need detailed knowledge of weather in order to go for a day sail. However, you do need to know what the weather will be doing during your trip. The key questions are:

- What wind and weather is here now and what is coming?
- How will it affect conditions, such as the sea state?
- What clothing should I wear and take with me?

There are many different sources of weather forecast:

Radio	Radio 4 Shipping Forecast and local radio
Coastguard	Marine safety information broadcast on VHF
Harbour office	Posted daily
Local sailing club	Posted daily
Smartphone	Via weather apps
Internet	Numerous sites including RYA website
Newspaper	General forecasts often with synoptic chart

Predicting the Sailing Conditions

It pays to think about how local effects will combine with the general weather. Think about your trip and what local effects there will be.

Northern Hemisphere

Low-pressure system – wind anticlockwise

- NE wind
- Wind follows direction of isobars
- SSE wind
- **LOW**
- Anticlockwise circulation
- Open isobars (less wind)
- Close isobars (more wind)
- **High-pressure system – wind clockwise**
- WNW wind
- S wind
- SSW wind
- NW wind
- **HIGH**
- Usually fair settled weather with high pressure
- Isolated squally showers behind cold front. Good visibility
- Drizzle
- SW wind
- Wind veer
- **Cold front**
- **Warm sector** Intermittent drizzle. Low cloud. Poor visibility
- **Warm front**
- SE wind

RYA Advanced Sailing   43

In general, if there are light gradient winds on the coast (the wind being due to a high- or low-pressure system) in any direction and there is a difference in temperature between sea and land, there is likely to be a sea breeze.

On a sunny day in particular the land heats up quickly, causing the air to rise. Replacement air is drawn in over the coastline – a sea breeze (fig. 1).

With a sea breeze in the same direction as the gradient wind, you may experience strong winds. Equally, if they are opposed and the gradient wind is strong, there may be a flat calm in the afternoon.

In general, the sea breeze will tend to veer (rotate with the sun) through the day, often ending up parallel to the coastline by sunset.

The wind will tend to accelerate as it funnels past the projections or obstructions, so an offshore breeze will most likely be turbulent and gusty (fig. 2).

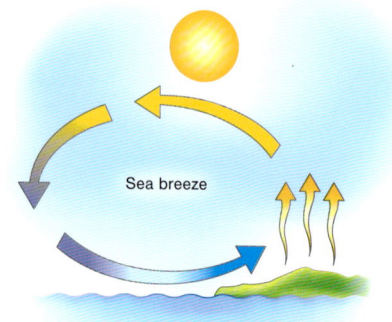

Fig. 1

Fig. 2

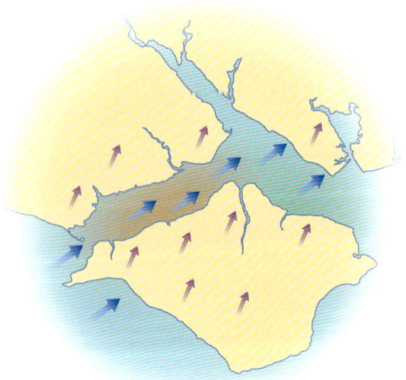

Over land, the wind is slowed and backed (deflected in the opposite direction to the sun), so if the wind is blowing parallel to the coast you may experience stronger or lighter winds depending on its direction.

For more information about weather and how to interpret synoptic charts etc., please refer to the *RYA Weather Handbook* (G133).

Tide-induced wind

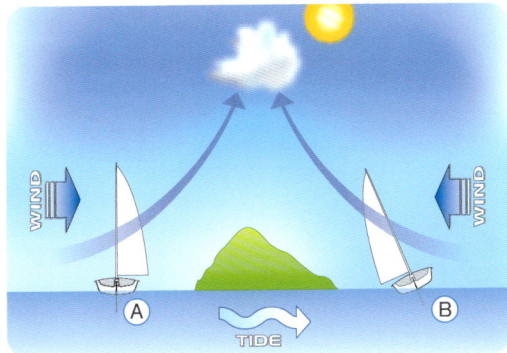

With no gradient wind, A and B are enjoying the sea breeze induced by a large island on a sunny day. A experiences less breeze as she moves in the tide. B is moved against the breeze and so feels more wind. Both boats will notice a difference when the tide turns. Wind and tide will have a considerable impact on sea conditions. Wind and tide directly opposed (wind over tide) can produce big waves with breaking tops, particularly in the entrance to an estuary mouth or over a sandbar. It pays to refer to an almanac or ask locally what conditions are likely.

Pilotage in Practice

Course to Steer

Although buoys mark channels, lining up two objects in transit is a very useful indication of a straight course.

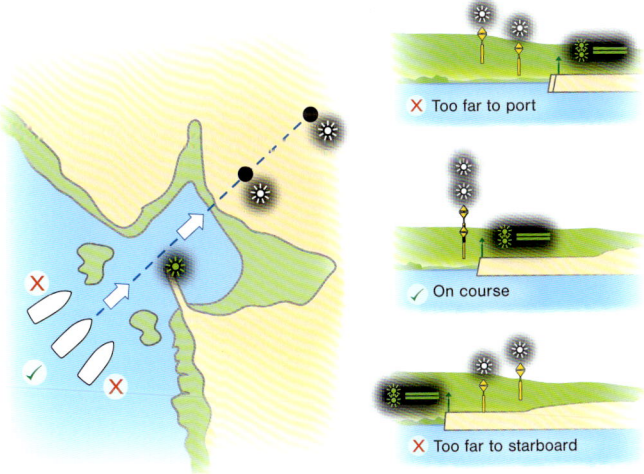

If you are unable to see your objective, use a compass to steer your course. However, using a compass in a small dinghy for pilotage during a day sail is not as useful as a good pilotage plan with regular identifiable marks. Compasses also suffer from deviation, caused by ferrous or electrical objects in the boat, so your course may not be that accurate.

You should also allow for the tidal flow and magnetic variation. If you look at the compass rose in the illustration it says 7 degrees. This is the magnetic variation we would use in our calculations if we set ourselves some compass headings.

Boat Speed

Boat speed is measured in knots, or nautical miles per hour. One knot is therefore slightly more than one mile per hour. With practice, you will be able to estimate your speed quite accurately. However, it will depend on the wind strength and direction on the day and whether the tidal flow is with or against you. There are various ways to measure speed and course over the ground which we will examine. See page 50.

Leeway

A small boat sailing to windward will naturally slide sideways, particularly in waves. Estimate leeway by comparing your wake with the course steered. When planning, allow for leeway. This is boat-specific and you may need to allow a considerable amount in certain conditions, like wind over tide when there are large waves, or in a small dinghy with a small centreboard.

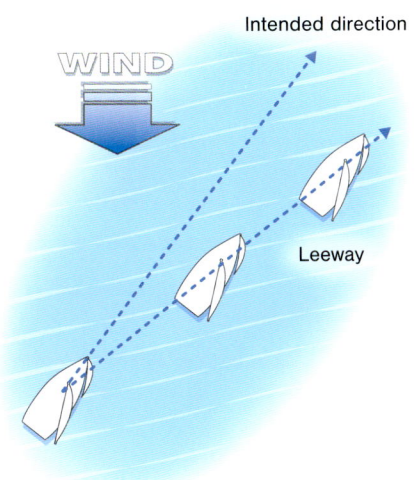

Tidal Flow

Some tidal streams around the UK are relatively strong and are therefore the major consideration when planning a trip. The level of the sea rises and falls as the tidal currents flow around the coast, resulting in two high tides and two low tides approximately every 25 hours. Your trip can be faster or slower, and the sea conditions will be affected by the tide.

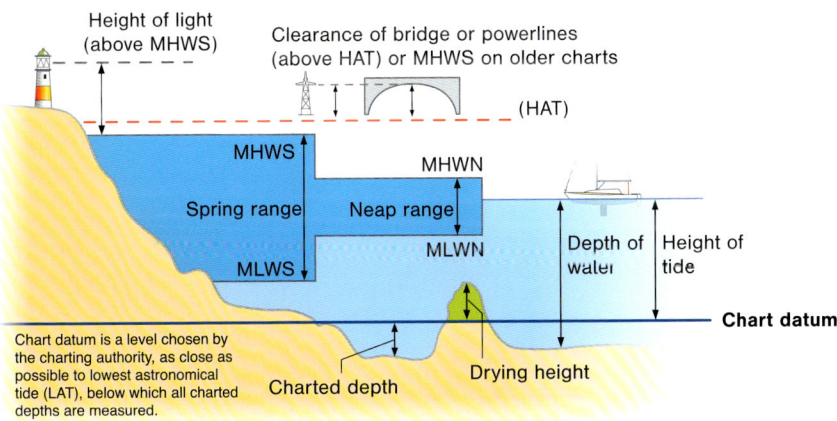

Note – Highest Astronomical Tide ('HAT') is replacing MHWS as the reference level for clearances – e.g. bridges and overhead electrical cables – as this represents the 'worst case' high tide and therefore the least clearance. Many charts though still reference these clearances to MHWS. Be careful to check the chart.

The critical questions to ask when planning your trip are:
- When does the tide change direction?
- How much flow is there in which direction?
- Is there sufficient depth for a safe course?

Times and heights of high and low water can be found in a nautical almanac. Local tide tables available from yacht chandlers, sailing clubs or the harbourmaster's office, or numerous smartphone apps provide all you need to know for local sailing. **Remember to correct for BST by adding one hour if necessary.**

The difference in height between each high water and the next low water is known as the tidal range.

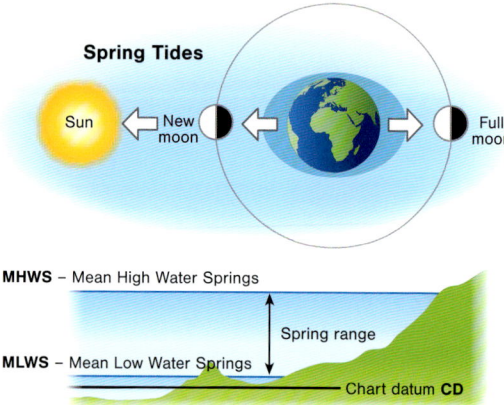

- Spring tides occur just after a full and new moon, and have a bigger range and therefore a stronger flow.

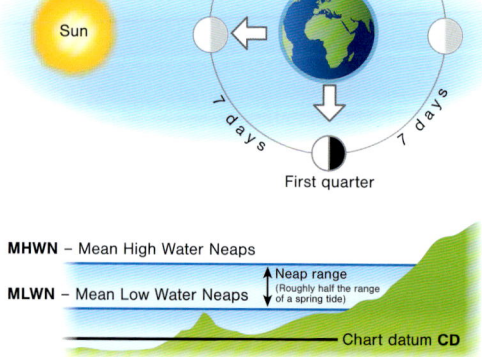

- Neap tides occur at half-moons and have a smaller range and hence a weaker flow.

48   RYA Advanced Sailing

In this example, the height of the evening tide varies between 1.1m and 3.4m above chart datum, a range of 2.3m.

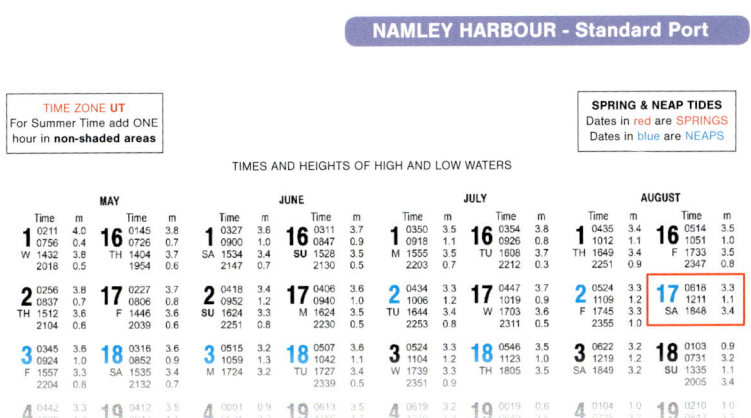

Though the tide does not necessarily turn at high or low water, the approximate height of tide can be worked out using either the Rule of Twelfths or the Rule of Percentages.

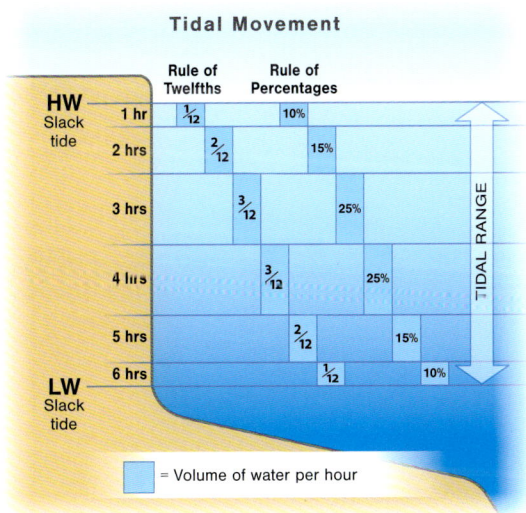

For a more accurate picture of flow rates, refer to the nearest tidal diamond on the chart, together with its associated table. Ensure you refer to the tide table for the correct standard port for your chart. Alternatively, refer to a tidal stream atlas. Both diamonds and atlases show the hourly flow and direction for spring and neap tides, together with the direction of flow.

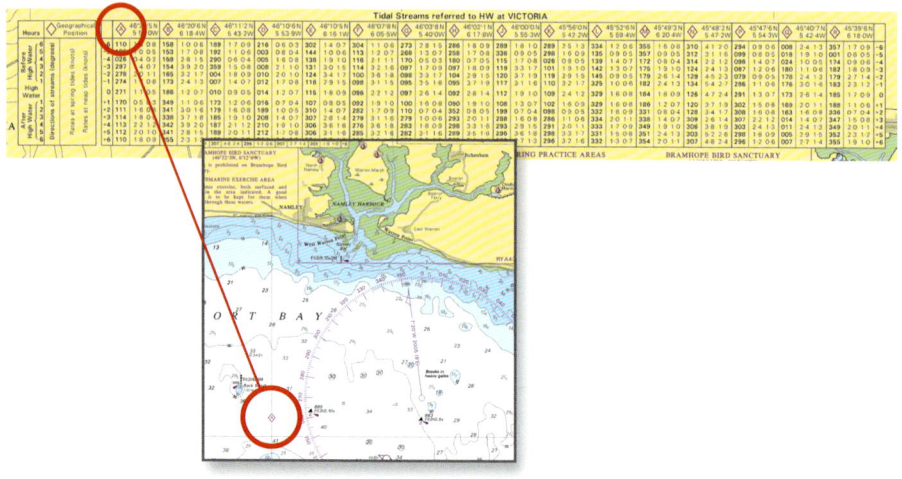

Pilotage with Global Positioning System (GPS)

A GPS receiver obtains a position fix from signals transmitted by orbiting satellites and is displayed on the GPS as latitude and longitude.

The simplest way to navigate with a GPS is to plot your latitude and longitude on a chart. A GPS set will give you much more information than this, though. For example, it will tell you your course and Speed over the Ground (SOG), and your position relative to a waypoint. As mentioned earlier, a GPS is a very accurate way of measuring boat speed.

Waypoints

Waypoints help you to navigate – they are positions that you can input and store in the memory of your GPS to use as reference points. When you activate a waypoint the GPS will display a lot of useful information that will help you fix your position and navigate to the waypoint. You can join a number of waypoints to create a route.

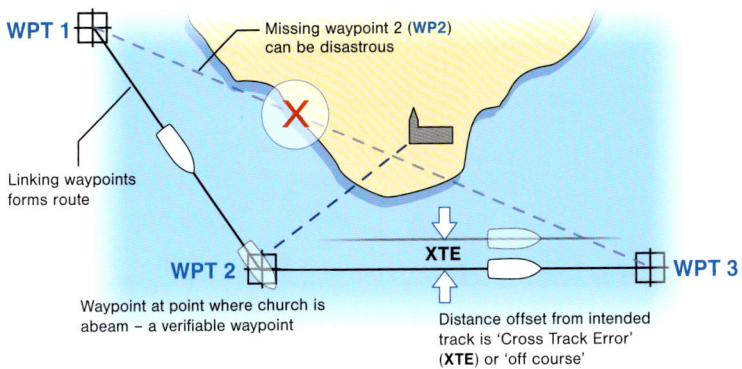

WPT 1 — Linking waypoints forms route
Missing waypoint 2 (WP2) can be disastrous
WPT 2 — Waypoint at point where church is abeam – a verifiable waypoint
XTE — Distance offset from intended track is 'Cross Track Error' (XTE) or 'off course'
WPT 3

Chart Plotter

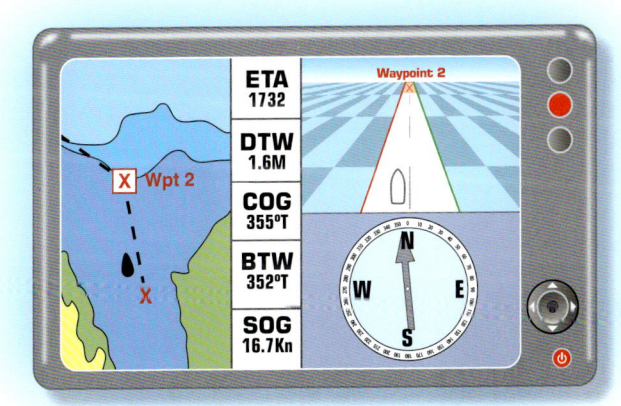

A chart plotter works in the same way as a GPS and it displays an overlay of a chart so you can see your course, speed and position in relation to hazards etc. It allows waypoints to be inserted and routes created, for example. A car's satellite navigation and various smartphone navigational apps are all examples of chart plotters where you see your position on a chart, giving course and speed etc.

Fixing your Position using a Waypoint

The GPS displays the range (distance) and bearing to a set waypoint. You can plot this directly on a chart using a plotter and pair of dividers. A more convenient way of obtaining a fix is to pre-draw a 'web' of bearings and distances to your chosen waypoint on a chart. When on your passage you can quickly compare the GPS display to the web. Matching your Course over the Ground (COG) to the bearing for a waypoint is a crude but useful way to stay on track. The GPS also uses your Speed Over the Ground (SOG) to calculate your Estimated Time of Arrival (ETA).

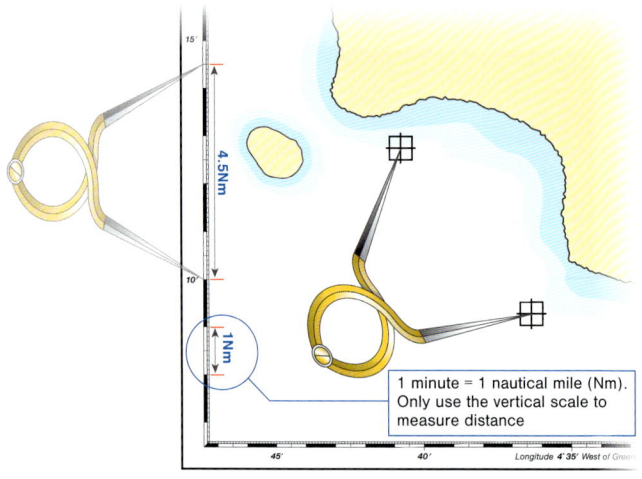

1 minute = 1 nautical mile (Nm). Only use the vertical scale to measure distance

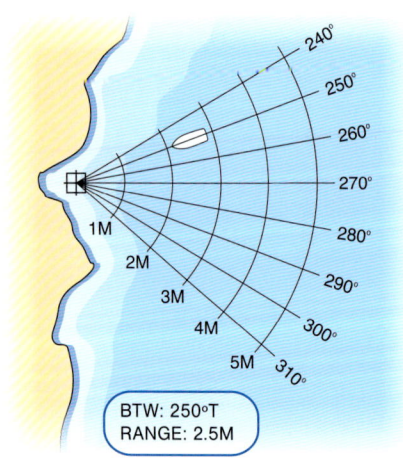

BTW: 250°T
RANGE: 2.5M

Navigating to a Waypoint

The GPS will also tell you your COG and SOG. Matching your COG to the bearing for a waypoint is a crude but useful way to stay on track.

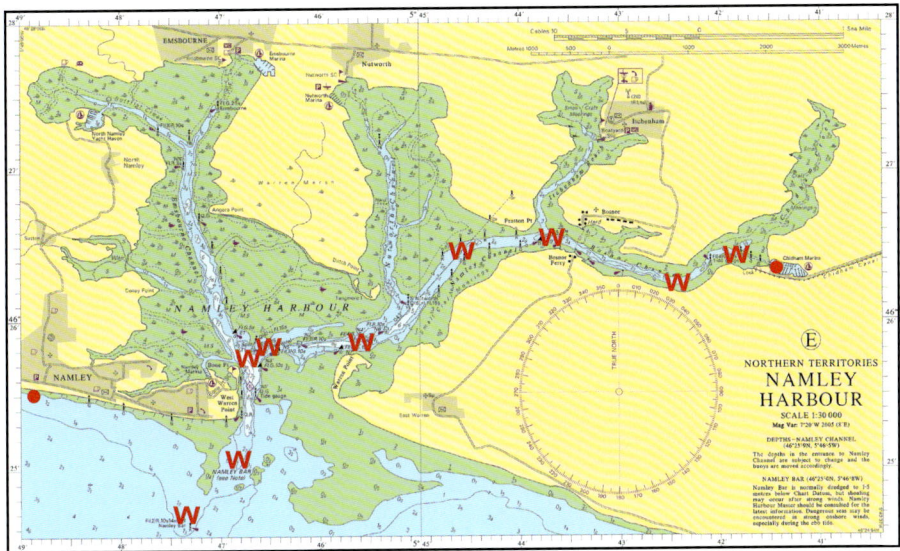

TOP TIP

Navigation by sat navs and plotters is generally reliable and accurate, but can go wrong due to lack of signal and limited battery life. Always back up your position with another source of information if you can, even if it's just a mark in your waterproof notebook on your route. Keep a record of your position.

Buoyage

The International Association of Lighthouse Authorities (IALA) 'A' system of buoyage is used throughout Europe. IALA B is used by countries in North, Central, and South America, Japan, Korea, and the Philippines. The system covers both lateral buoyage (marking the sides of the channels) and cardinal buoyage (marking hazards or navigational features relative to compass direction). The buoyage system is designed principally for larger vessels and is useful for navigation and pilotage. The book G2 *RYA International Regulations for Preventing Collisions at Sea* is a great source of information for buoyage and navigation.

IALA A

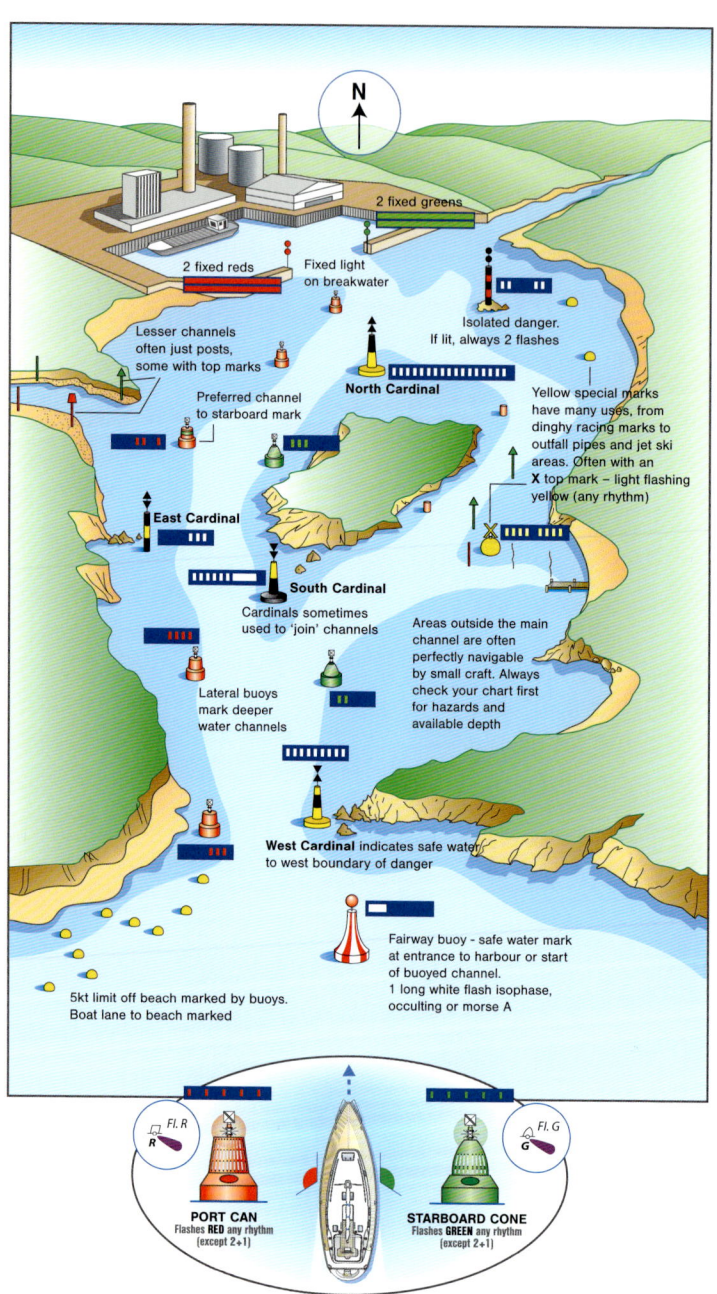

IALA B

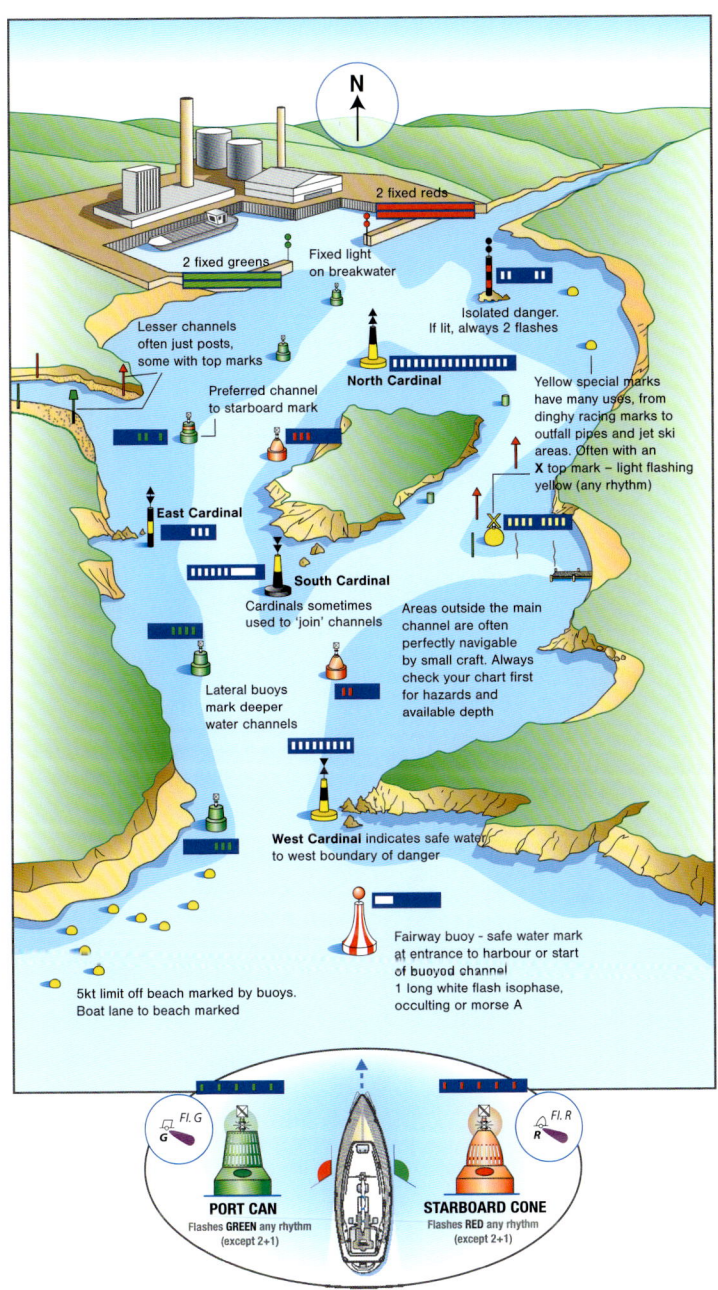

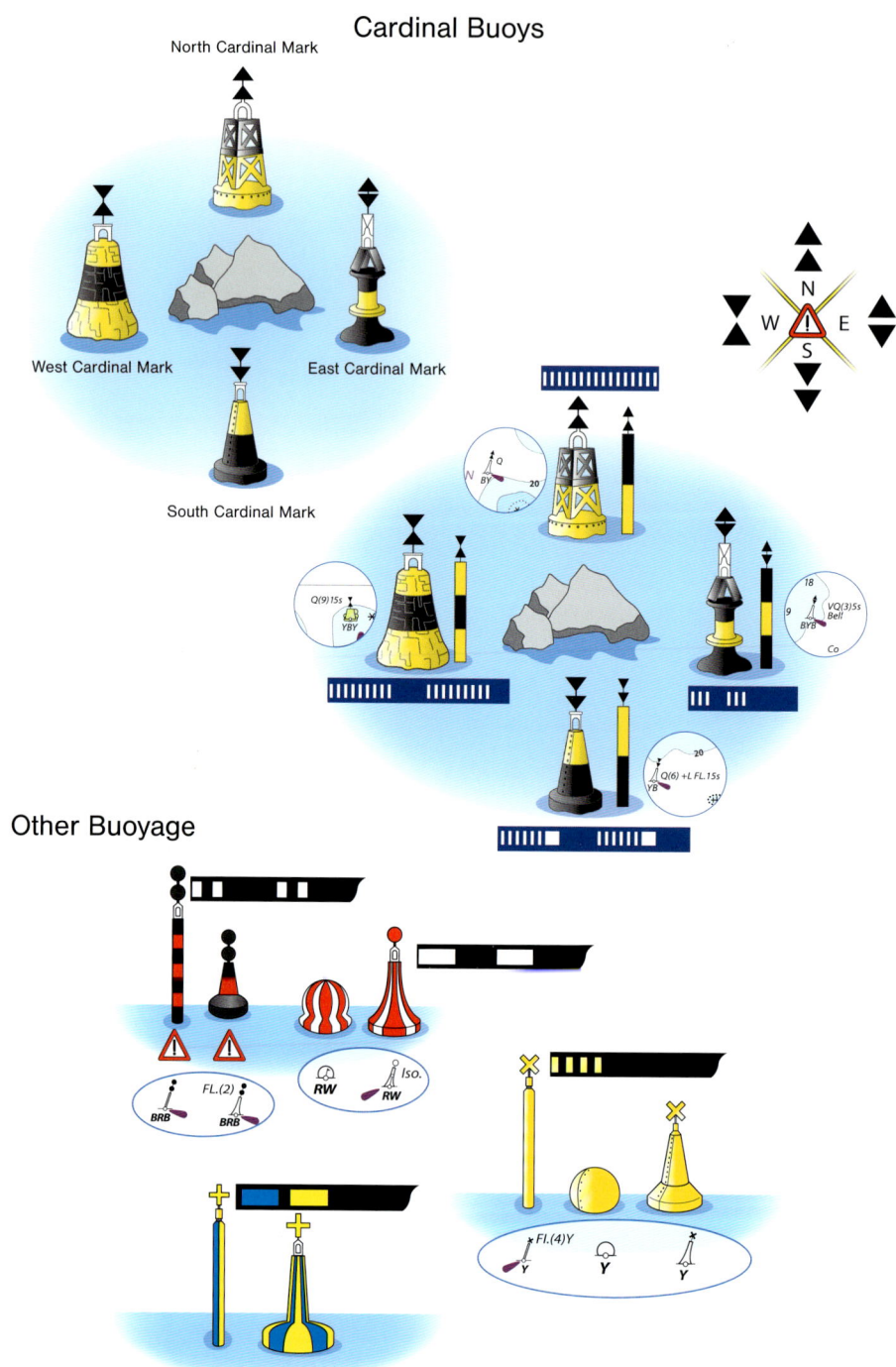

Channel Marks

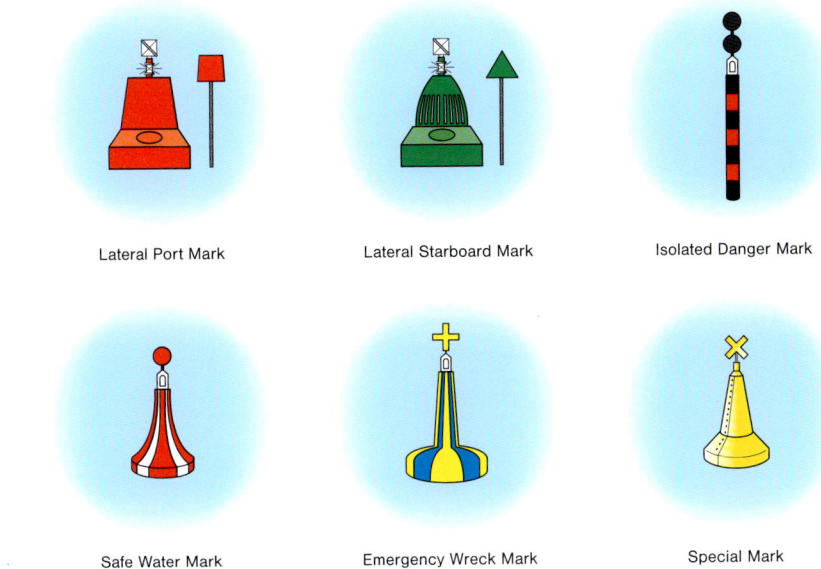

Lateral Port Mark

Lateral Starboard Mark

Isolated Danger Mark

Safe Water Mark

Emergency Wreck Mark

Special Mark

Preferred Channel Marks

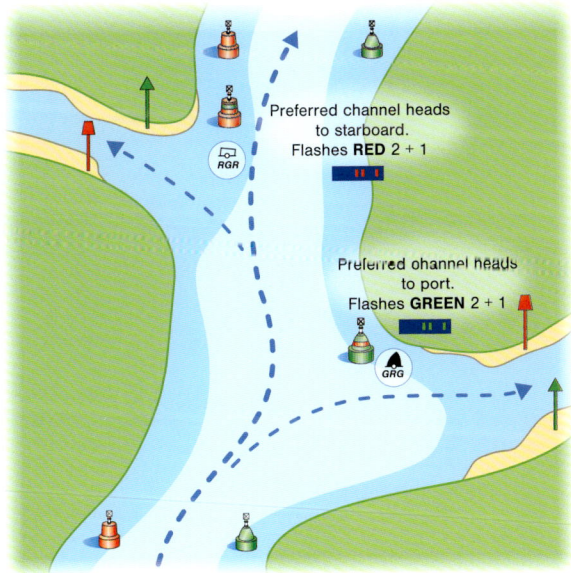

Landing on a Shore

If you are cruising in a dinghy or shallow keelboat (bilge or lifting keel), you may well wish to go ashore at some point. Beware that if land is privately owned there may be no right of access above the high-water mark.

If the wind is at least slightly offshore you may be able to take the anchor up the beach, leaving the boat afloat. This will depend on any tidal stream. Plan for what will happen if the tide turns while you are ashore.

If you choose a lee shore, either sail ashore under jib only and lift the boat ashore or anchor close offshore and ease the boat back into shallow water to make your landing. Again, beware of the tide. A change in the conditions may result in the boat swinging out of reach once you are ashore, so consider taking a stern line ashore. To depart, simply climb aboard, hoist the sails and haul off using the anchor, as long as you haven't let the boat dry out. More information can be found in the Seamanship chapter.

Estimating the Height of Tide (HOT)

The height of tide at any time can be estimated reasonably accurately using one of two rules. The idea is to estimate the amount that the tide has accumulated or fallen in each hour. The flow accelerates and decelerates so the amount of water accumulated each hour is different. Note that you should still leave a margin for error.

This example refers to our expected trip day, 17 August, on the Namley Harbour tide table.

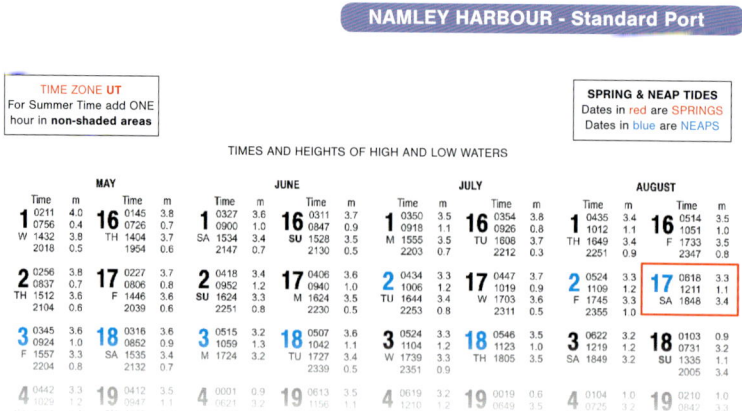

From the tide table, on 17 August the range after the morning high water is:

HW=3.3 - LW=1.1 = 2.2m

For the Percentage Rule:

10 per cent of range = 10 per cent of 2.2 = 0.22m.

For the Rule of Twelfths:

1/12 of range = 1/12 of 2.2m = 0.183m, say 0.18m

To obtain an approximate depth at any time, add the Height of Tide (HOT) to the depth indicated on the chart at that point. As mentioned earlier, this could be a drying height on the chart and adding the HOT to this still may not give enough water to sail.

So, for example, two hours after high water, the depth at any charted point can be estimated by taking the HOT at high water and subtracting the amount of water which has flowed away. This will be 25 per cent or 3/12 of the range.

So on 17 August where HW of 2.1m is indicated on the chart, depth at HW-2 hours of ebb tide = 2.1 - (0.18 (1st hour 1/12) + 0.36 (2nd hour 2/12)) = 1.56m using the Rule of Twelfths.

Sample Plan for a Day Sail

Step 1: Decide on your trip and obtain tidal and weather information

Tom wants to explore the estuary in his dinghy or keelboat starting from Chidham Marina where he stores his boat. He exits Namley Harbour and sails west along the coast to the parking area on the foreshore in Namley, a distance of approximately 6 nautical miles. Local high water at Namley is around 0618hrs and 1848 hrs, but Tom will need to look at the high-water times for Victoria because the tidal diamonds on the chart refer to that port. High water at Victoria on 17 August is around 0506hrs and 1750hrs.

⬨ B	46°25'6 N 5 46·7W	
183	0·8	0·5
178	0·4	0·2
003	0·9	0·4
005	1·7	0·9
007	2·0	1·0
004	1·6	0·8
003	1·1	0·6
002	0·5	0·3
179	0·6	0·4
180	1·6	0·8
181	2·2	1·2
182	1·9	1·0
184	1·4	0·7

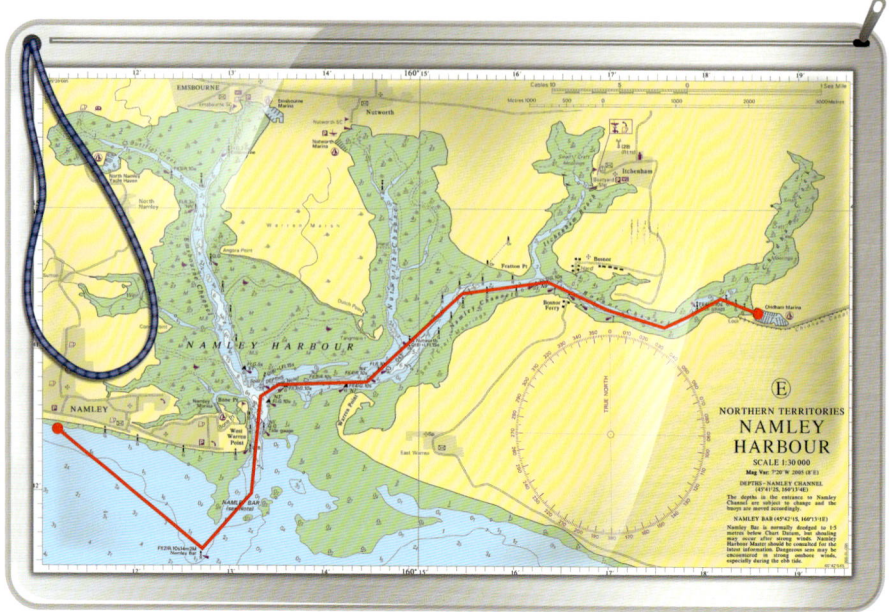

The weather forecast is southerly Force 2 becoming southerly Force 3. It is bright and sunny; local knowledge suggests that the sea breeze will increase this to Force 4 veering to the south-west in the late afternoon.

The nearest high water at Namley to his proposed departure time on 17 August is 0618hrs (UT), corrected to 0718hrs BST, say 0720hrs BST. The most appropriate tidal diamond to use for the tidal stream is 'B', as it is located in the area of his passage at the most tidal area, the entrance and exit to Namley Harbour. The corrected time to work out the tidal streams from tidal diamond 'B' for Victoria HW is 0606hrs BST (say 0600hrs) and 1850hrs BST.

The tidal flows listed for tidal diamond B shows that the tidal flow will carry him west from Chidham Marina as the tide ebbs out of the harbour, then south out through the entrance of Namley Harbour from 0830hrs to 1400hrs BST. Tom plans to sail west along the coast until sometime between 1300hrs BST and 1400hrs BST. The tidal flow starts to re-enter the harbour at 1430hrs and continues to flood north (at the entrance) and east towards Chidham Marina for the rest of the day. Tom could also have obtained the same information from a tidal stream atlas or smartphone app.

Step 2: Predict the conditions you will experience

Tom is confident sailing in the estuary but concerned about the exit through the entrance to Namley Harbour as the almanac predicts rough water in a southerly breeze during spring ebbs. During Tom's predicted passage the wind and tide are opposed until the tide turns, so he expects a choppy sea in the morning, but as the wind is light it should only be a small chop. When the tide turns in the afternoon for the return trip, the seas will flatten as the wind and tide are together, making it a pleasant return trip to Chidham Marina. Visibility will be moderate, so for safety he decides to carry a radio as well as flares and looks at safe havens along the route. He selects Bosnor Ferry, Warren Point and West Warren Point. He also looks in the almanac and makes a note of the VHF channels to call the Harbour Master, Namely Marina and Bosnor Ferry.

NAMLEY HARBOUR – Standard Port

46°25'.74N 005°46'.70W
Northern Territories CHARTS RYA 3, 4.

Standard Port NAMLEY HARBOUR (→)

Times				Height (metres)			
High Water		Low Water		MHWS	MHWN	MLWN	MLWS
0000	0600	0000	0600	4.0	3.4	1.1	0.4
1200	1800	1200	1800				
Differences ITCHENHAM							
+0020	+0010	-0005	0000	-0.2	-0.1	-0.1	-0.1
Differences EMSBOURNE							
+0010	+0010	-0010	-0005	-0.3	-0.1	0.0	-0.1

DESCRIPTION. The harbour provides very good shelter in the various channels, creeks and marinas. There are five marinas and numerous visitors' moorings along the channels. Hbr speed limit of 8kn. Hbr staff do prosecute for speeding offences; they also prosecute sailing vessels for failing to display a motoring cone when motor sailing.

APPROACH WAYPOINT. 46°24'.41N 005°47'.08W.

PILOTAGE NOTES. APPROACHES: Leave the Bar Beacon [Fl(2)R.10s14m2M] (H bn) 50m to port, as the channel N'ward is only 100m wide. It is advisable to select a transit ahead to check for drift to avoid being swept onto the shoals that flank the entrance. Leaving the tide gauge (Q.G) to stbd, make towards the SCM where the channel divides N towards Emsbourne and ENE towards Itchenham. Depths may change in this area and the buoys will be moved accordingly; the HM should be consulted for the latest information. Both main channels are well marked with buoys. Do not enter or leave harbour during onshore gales as dangerous conditions may be encountered, especially with a spring ebb.

TIDAL STREAMS AND HEIGHTS. Best entry/exit is HW -3 to HW +1 avoiding the confused seas caused by the strong ebb stream. During spring tides, the bar becomes very uncomfortable in onshore winds > F5 combined with the ebb stream. The bar is dredged to 1.5m below CD but this may vary by ±0.75m after heavy onshore gales.

LIGHTS AND MARKS. Namley Bar Beacon [Fl(2)R.10s14m2M] is a conspicuous red painted wooden structure. A weather station on the beacon www.namleymetstn.co.nt gives access to the current weather conditions in the vicinity of the entrance. All channels within the harbour are well marked by day. Emsbourne and Namley Channels are partly lit. Nutworth Channel and Itchenham Reach are unlit.

VHF RADIO. Namley Harbour Radio and patrol vessels VHF Ch **14**, 16. Marinas VHF Ch 80.

FACILITIES. Clockwise from W Warren Point:
Namley Marina. 30 V. Access at all states of the tide via dredged channel 2m; pontoons have 1.6m. ME, El, P, D, M, Gas, CH, C (25 tonnes). From Bone Point SC follow marked channel to marina. **North Namley Yacht Haven**. 20 V. 1.3m channel to marina. Access HW -5 to +4 ½ ME, El, FW, BH (10 tonnes) **Emsbourne Marina**. 10 V. Approach channel dries 0.5m. Access HW +2 over 1.0m sill, which maintains 1.7m inside. Slip, FW, Gas, CH, ME, El, BH (60 tonnes), C (20 tonnes). **Nutworth Marina**. 6 V. Drying 0.5m in approach channel and berths. FW, P&D (cans), Bar, R. There is a public slipway at Nutworth SC. **Chidham Marina**. 20 V. Enter well-marked channel to lock. Channel is dredged to CD. A waiting pontoon is outside the lock. Call Lock Keeper on Ch 80 and await G light. Free flow near HW times. **Itchenham**. Unmarked channel, stay close to moored vessels. AB (drying 1.0m), FW, BY, ME, El, BH (10 tonnes), Slip.

Step 3: Predict how long each part of the passage will take

This will be a combination of the boat's speed and direction with the tidal flow and direction. On the outward journey Tom's boat can sail (boat speed) at up to 6 knots reaching from Chidham Marina to Bone Point. He then has to beat out of the harbour, and this will reduce his speed to 4 knots. He expects to manage only 3–4 knots in the conditions. The return journey will be slightly quicker as there will be no beat and Tom may be able to hoist the spinnaker.

If he leaves at 1000hrs BST he will be on the maximum favourable tide of between 1.2 to 1.0 knots until the tide turns between 1300hrs BST and 1400hrs BST.

Tom should therefore reach the Namley parking spot comfortably, have time to go ashore, have a picnic and a walk around before the tide turns and assists him back to Chidham Marina on the flood tide.

He can explore Namley on a low tide before his departure back to Chidham Marina. The expected breeze in the afternoon will be in the same direction as the tide, making for a calm, swift passage into the harbour, where tidal flow will become stronger during the afternoon, and help Tom sail back to the marina. He can check the height of tide using the method shown earlier if he thinks he will arrive too early.

Having stopped for his picnic and explored a little, Tom reckons he might set off at 1400hrs BST. The tidal diamond shows a tidal stream of between 0.4 knots when he starts, increasing to 1.0 knots north and east until 0230hrs BST on the 18th. By then the wind may be veering to the south-west. Sea conditions will be very calm, making it a gentler journey than the outward trip. Tom will take off some of the extra clothing he wore for the trip out, stow it securely in the boat and make sure everything is stowed correctly.

In the afternoon, with the forecasted fresher breeze, Tom decides to reef, estimating that his boat speed will still be about 4 knots. He will be reaching and running into the harbour, assisted by the flood tide, so his speed over the ground should be 4 knots plus tide of 1.0 knots = 5.0 knots SOG with little leeway.

Achieving 6.0 nautical miles easily before 1700hrs BST ensures that he should cover the 6 nautical miles comfortably before the tide turns again at 1848hrs (UT) or 1948hrs BST, say 1950hrs local time.

When does the tide turn?

The tidal diamond information refers to 30 minutes each side of the indicated time:

Published Data:			Means:		
1200	044	0.5	1130hrs BST–1230hrs BST	044°	0.5 knots
1300	046	0.1	1230hrs BST–1330hrs BST	046°	0.1 knots
1400	214	0.5	1330hrs BST–1430hrs BST	214°	0.5 knots

So, in this example, the tide turns from north-east to south-west at 1330hrs BST. There will, of course, be a period of slack water but the tidal diamonds sometimes do not show this clearly.

Information used from Victoria Tidal Diamond ('B') for planning the trip:

Published Data:				Numbers used for planning trip:		
Time:	Direction:	Rate of flow:		Time:	Direction:	Speed used:
		Springs	Neaps		(Neaps)	
-6	183°	0.8	0.5	1230 BST–1330 BST	183°	0.5m knots
-5	178°	0.4	0.2	1330 BST–1430 BST	178°	0.2 knots
-4	003°	0.9	0.4	1430 BST–1530 BST	003°	0.4 knots
-3	005°	1.7	0.9	1530 BST–1630 BST	005°	0.9 knots
-2	007°	2.0	1.0	1630 BST–1730 BST	007°	1.0 knot
-1	004°	1.6	0.8	1730 BST–1830 BST	004°	0.8 knots
HW 0506	003°	1.1	0.6			
+1	002°	0.5	0.3			
+2	179°	0.6	0.4	0830 BST–0930 BST	179°	0.4 knots
+3	180°	1.6	0.8	0930 BST–1030 BST	180°	0.8 knots
+4	181°	2.2	1.2	0930 BST–1030 BST	181°	1.2 knots
+5	182°	1.9	1.0	1030 BST–1130 BST	182°	1.0 knots
+6	184°	1.4	0.7	1130 BST–1230 BST	184°	0.7 knots

Step 4: Alternatives

The inward journey should be predictable even with the predicted wind strengthening. As the tide is flooding, the wind and tide are together so the sea will be flat, and Tom will reef to reduce power. However, the wind and tide in the morning could make the sail out through the entrance to Namley Harbour a bit choppy. Therefore Tom plans to wear more clothing, stows the equipment well and can abort the trip if he feels continuing out through the entrance is too difficult. If conditions are too rough, Tom plans simply to turn around early and broad reach back to Chidham Marina, but could call into Western Point for his picnic and walk before the tide turns and he can have a short sail to Chidham Marina.

Though no overfalls (rough seas) are shown on the chart, it would be wise to approach the exit and entrance to the harbour with caution in case there are strong tidal eddies as mentioned in the almanac.

On the other hand, if the sea breeze does not materialise due to cloudy weather, Tom may find the breeze remains southerly and have an easy return trip with the tide behind him.

Tom has also looked at boltholes and selected Bosnor Ferry, Warren Point and Bone Point along the way if anything happens.

GOLDEN RULE

Always leave details with a reliable person of your boat, the numbers aboard, route and expected time of return.

Tom also notes from the almanac that he should take a good transit when leaving and returning through the harbour entrance as there could be sideways drift. The best entry and exit is between HW -03 and HW +1 to miss confused seas caused by strong ebb streams. Tom also makes a note that the harbour and patrol VHF radio frequencies are channels 14 and 16, and that the marinas are on channel 80. The channel for navigating is well marked and dredged to chart datum (CD).

Tom finalises his plan, identifies his transits for the critical points, and copies it into his waterproof notebook. Tom also places some waypoints into his smartphone, waterproofs his chart, and makes a copy of everything. Tom arranges to leave this copy with the Chidham Marina lock keeper as emergency backup. Tom also agrees to do a radio

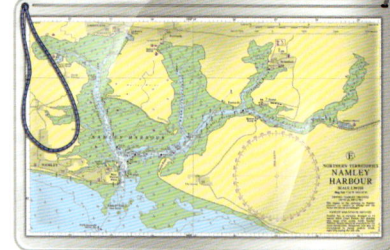

check with the lock keeper prior to leaving for his trip, and also provides a contact number in case of emergencies.

Tom is ready for his trip and starts to track the local weather in the weeks running up to it. He begins to make sure his boat is ready, checks his running and standing rigging and sails, and gets a spares pack ready.

Decision-making during a Passage

Remember to leave details of your trip with a reliable person ashore and inform them of any change in plans. In this way you can be sure of the alarm being raised if you are late. If strong winds are forecast, or if you are caught out by too much/too little wind or bad weather, have an alternative plan ready and make decisions early. Remember that the sea state may change dramatically when the tide turns, so keep a generous margin for error. Plan ahead, asking yourself how you would deal with different eventualities. It is wise to pre-plan 'boltholes' in case of emergencies along your expected route.

Passages in Strong Winds

When sailing in strong winds or waves, pay close attention to the 'five essentials': boat balance, trim, sail setting, centreboard and course made good.

- Reduce sail area or depower the rig early rather than late – sailing at top speed may be thrilling but you can quickly become tired and make mistakes.
- Concentrate on balancing the boat and trim to stay dry – if your dinghy is punching into a heavy sea and water is coming into the boat, move back a little to lift the bow.
- Think carefully about where to sail for a sheltered passage or a more favourable tide.
- Look out for confused water, indicating strong tides or shallow water.
- Keep an eye out for other boats.
- Above all, make safe, seamanlike and conservative decisions.

4 SAILING WITH SPINNAKERS

Over the years, dinghy and catamaran sailing has undergone a number of far-reaching changes.

In the 1930s, Uffa Fox introduced planing dinghies. In the 1960s, the ability to plane to windward was developed. In the 1980s, Julian Bethwaite developed the asymmetric spinnaker and completed the logical gybing-downwind technique. Some of these developments have evolved through lighter equipment and better materials, some through better techniques.

As dinghies have got faster, theory and practice for dinghies, catamarans and windsurfers have merged. High-performance dinghy sailing now takes place in apparent wind, just as it does for high-performance catamarans and planing windsurfers.

This chapter looks at the impact of apparent wind while planing downwind, and the difference between conventional (symmetric) and asymmetric spinnakers.

TOP TIP

The lighter and faster the dinghy, the greater the relevance of apparent wind.

Steering

As soon as the maximum righting force is exerted on a boat, by hiking or trapezing, steering controls the boat's balance. With a spinnaker flying, modern rigs develop tremendous power. To control any excess power (sailing in the power zone), helms should bear away, thereby reducing the heeling moment (balance) on the boat.

To steer positively, keep the tiller extension as close as possible to a right angle with the tiller. Consider where you are sitting in the boat and change your steering style to suit, either pan handle or dagger grip.

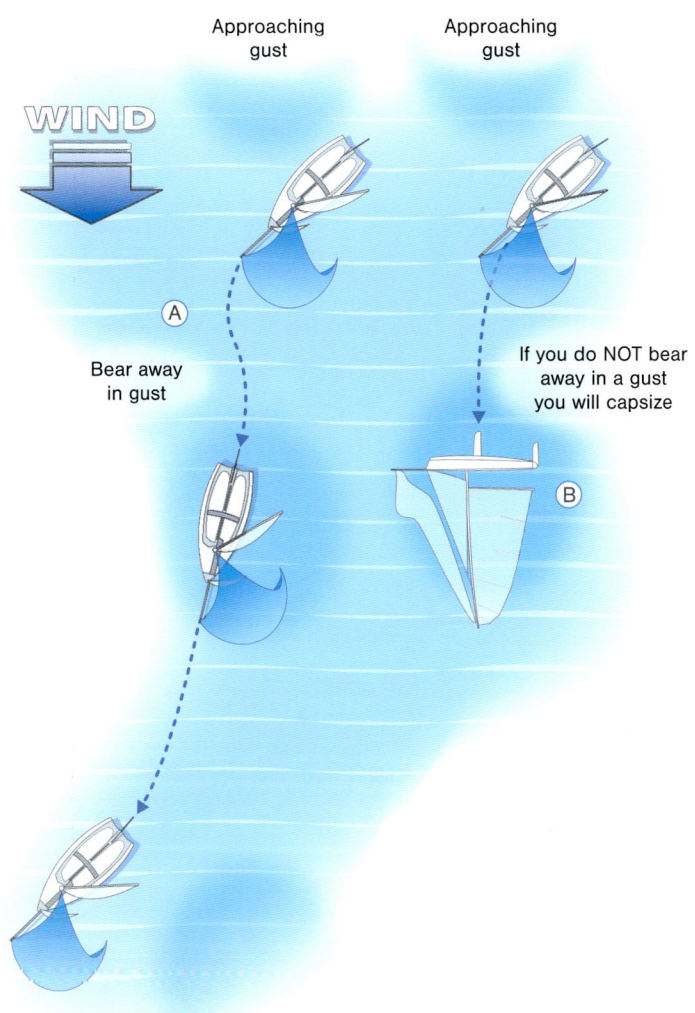

GOLDEN RULE

Steering controls power when sailing downwind. Bear away in gusts and luff up in the lulls to keep the boat level.

Conventional (Symmetric) and Asymmetric Spinnakers

The conventional spinnaker was developed to gain better speed downwind. With the heeling forces greatly reduced when going downwind, it was possible to fly this specialist sail while running and gain considerable speed without excessive heeling. Originally only flown on runs, sailors soon developed the skill of sailing slightly higher to gain speed by flying the spinnaker on a broad reach.

As sailors in the development classes were at the forefront of these changes it was no surprise to see more specialist sails being created by the Australian 18-foot class. Races were won by gybing conventional spinnakers downwind and sailing much greater distances (Course Made Good (CMG)) at a significant speed advantage (Velocity Made Good (VMG)) in these planing hulls.

Eventually, this led to the creation of an asymmetric spinnaker, which was not only better suited to sailing higher angles but also simplified the spinnaker systems.

Instead of controlling the height and angle of the conventional pole, the entire technique was changed to hoisting, gybing and dropping the spinnaker from a fixed pole. Because the gybing pole was replaced with a single, central pole, gybing had become as easy as swapping the jib from starboard to port or vice versa. As a result of these developments, there is a clear choice in the performance-boat market between boats with different types of spinnaker, each with its own strengths and weaknesses.

TOP TIP

Flying any spinnaker will need strong communication between helm and crew.

Stowage

The spinnaker (conventional or asymmetric) is stowed in either a bag or a chute. The chute option is the easiest to control as the spinnaker can be retrieved into the boat by pulling on the downhaul (retrieval) line and storing the spinnaker in the chute sock.

Rigging Tips

Tie the spinnaker sheets together to stop ends tangling and allow better control when gybing. Tape the loose ends. On asymmetric spinnakers, make sure the attachment to the sail is as small as possible so it can be pulled around the front of the jib. Special knots have been designed.

TOP TIP

Always fly your spinnaker before going afloat. To check an asymmetric, start at the tack, run up the luff to the head, then down the leech to the clew. Check that the spinnaker sheets go round the jib and are over the retrieval line.

Asymmetric Spinnaker Handling

Once hoisted, the sail develops a lot of power, so steering is the key. The steering must balance the forces on the boat. The crew cannot move into the boat until the sideways force is decreased by steering the boat away from the wind (see power zone diagram below).

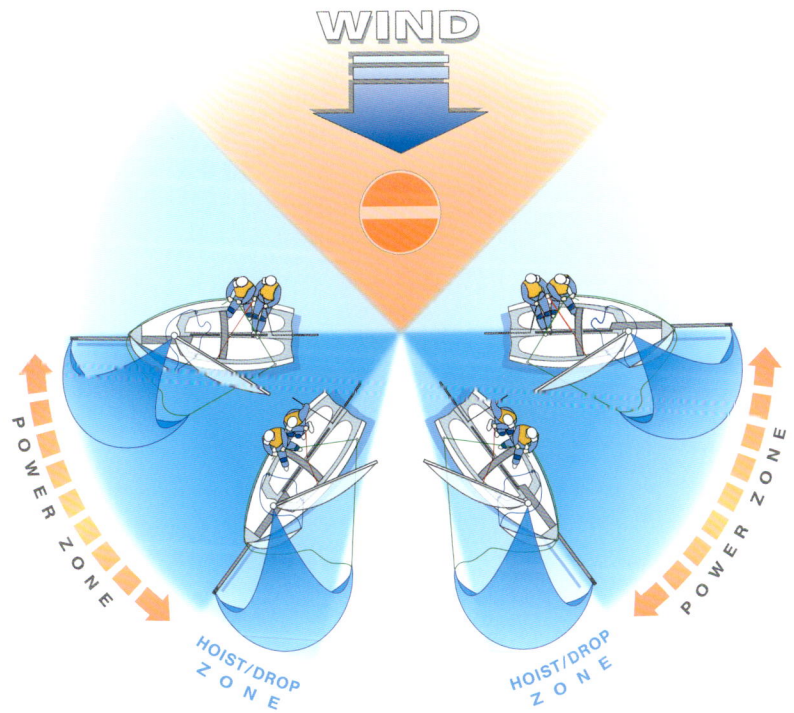

To hoist, gybe or drop, bear away into the hoist/drop zone to decrease the power on the boat. The exact angle needed will be wind and boat dependent.

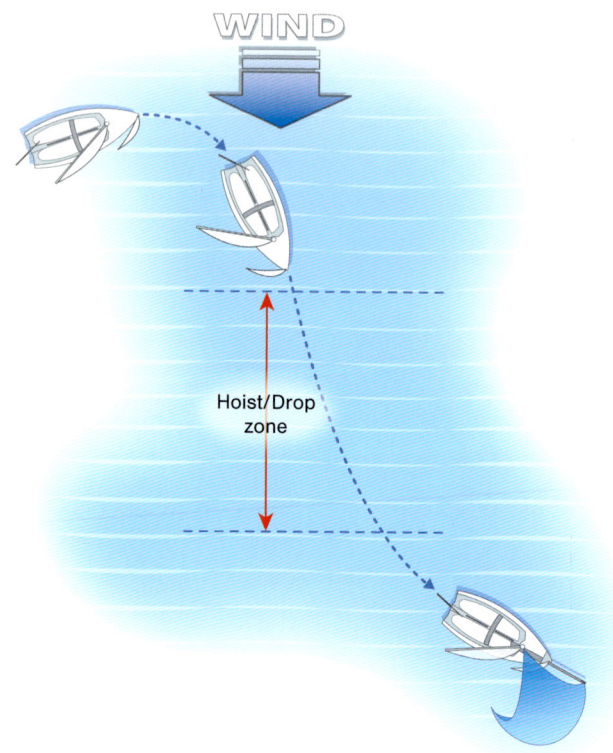

The stronger the wind and the faster the boat, the lower we can sail. Very fast boats in a Force 5 will almost be running in order to decrease the load and allow the crew to go into the boat to hoist the spinnaker.

1. When turning from a beat to a broad reach you will go through an area (at about beam reach) where the forces will increase.
2. In strong winds, bear away through this zone as quickly as possible.
3. Once on a broad reach/run and in the hoist/drop zone the crew can hoist the spinnaker.
4. Depending on the boat, there may be one halyard that deploys the pole as well as hoists the spinnaker, or two. The pole should be launched first if they are separate.

5. Hoist as quickly as possible.

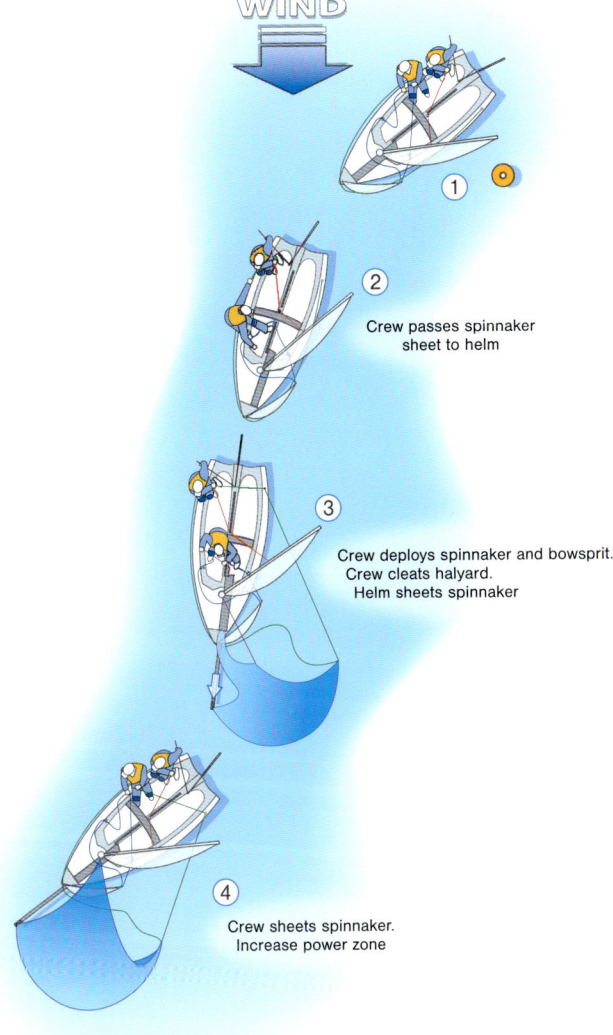

Crew passes spinnaker sheet to helm

Crew deploys spinnaker and bowsprit.
Crew cleats halyard.
Helm sheets spinnaker

Crew sheets spinnaker.
Increase power zone

6. If the spinnaker gets caught in a wave, quickly hoist it up out of the water before the boat slows down. Once the spinnaker is hoisted, the helm turns the boat higher into the wind (entering the power zone) and exposes the spinnaker (which has until now been blanketed by the mainsail).
7. At the same time, the crew sheets in the spinnaker until it fills, then immediately eases the sail until the luff starts to curl (see Trimming).

As the boat accelerates, the crew and helm either hike or trapeze to balance the forces on the boat. The higher you sail (steering) the more balance is needed to offset the heeling forces. The spinnaker and mainsail must be trimmed correctly, otherwise the boat will not accelerate and the forces on it will quickly build and generate large amounts of heel which will decrease the speed. If the spinnaker has an 'hourglass' twist after hoisting, try gybing to free it.

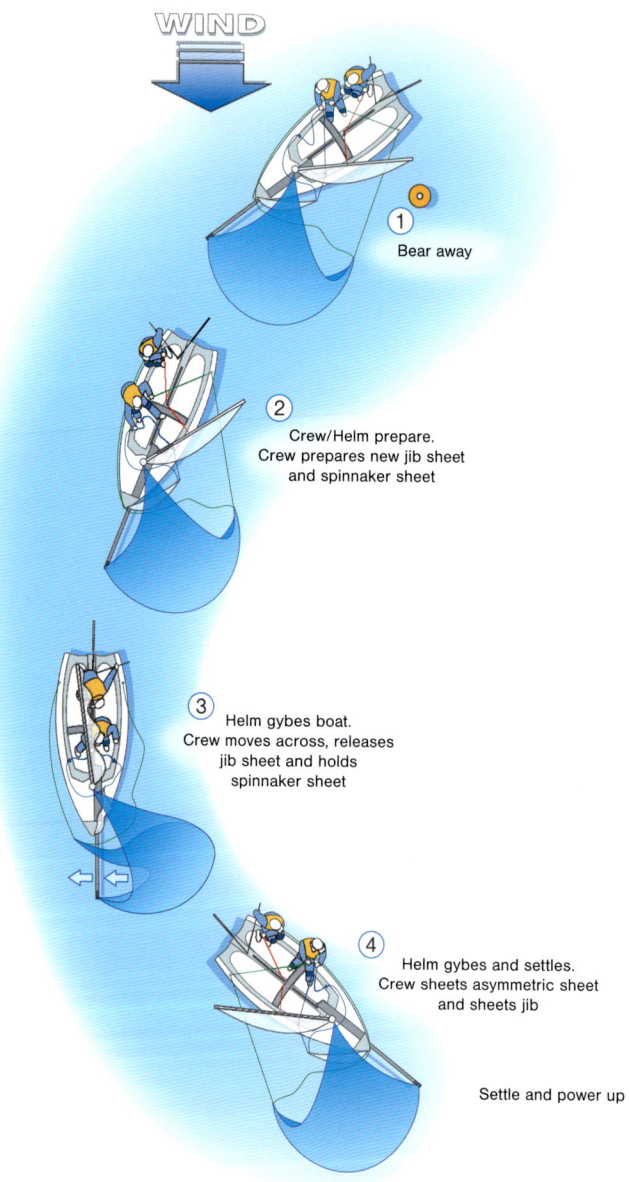

1. Bear away

2. Crew/Helm prepare. Crew prepares new jib sheet and spinnaker sheet

3. Helm gybes boat. Crew moves across, releases jib sheet and holds spinnaker sheet

4. Helm gybes and settles. Crew sheets asymmetric sheet and sheets jib

Settle and power up

72   RYA Advanced Sailing

Trimming

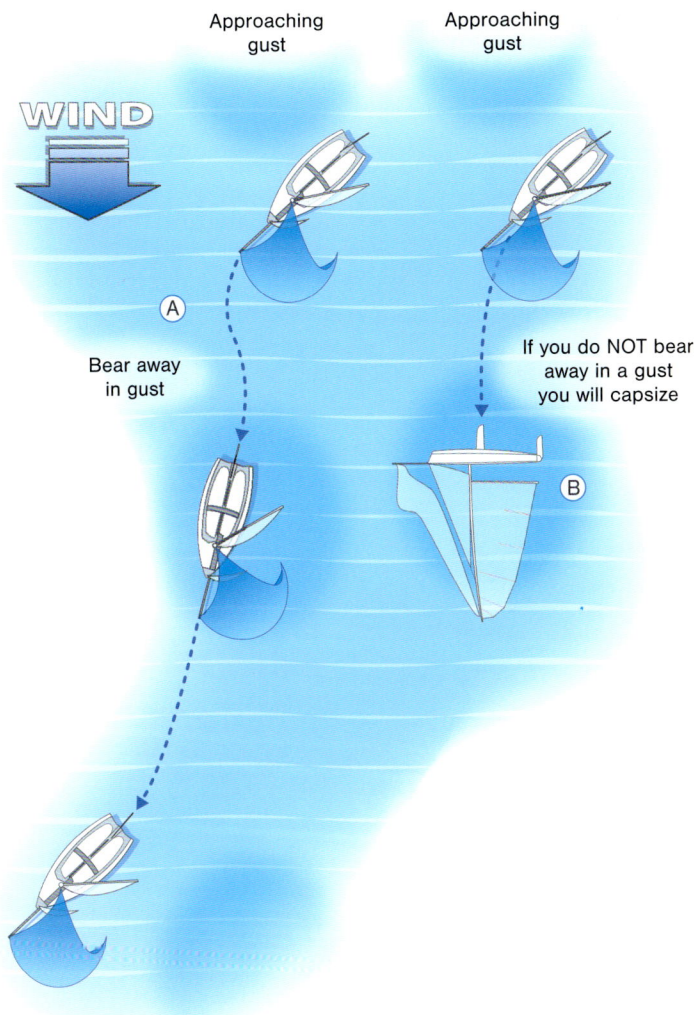

To trim asymmetric spinnakers, concentrate on the luff of the sail. Ease the sheet until the sail starts to roll over (approximately six inches) and then gently sheet in to roll it back.

By repeating this procedure constantly on the downwind leg the spinnaker will always be trimmed at the optimum angle to the wind. Communication between crew and helm is important.

Steering and Balance

With the crew constantly looking at and trimming the spinnaker, the helm controls the balance by steering. If you are overpowered and start to heel, simply bear away. Likewise, if you are in a lull you can increase power by steering higher. Each different design of dinghy will have an optimum angle for the conditions and this is where experience of a particular design pays.

To gain this knowledge, experiment against similar boats or attend class association training weekends.

The skill is to spot the gust and anticipate the extra sideways force as it lands, bearing away as the boat accelerates. Note that with large spinnakers the effect of moving body weight further out will be minimal.

TOP TIP

When racing fast boats you may have to sail higher and further to induce planing. You should make a gain over other boats not planing as the apparent wind builds and heads (VMG v. CMG).

Gybing the Spinnaker

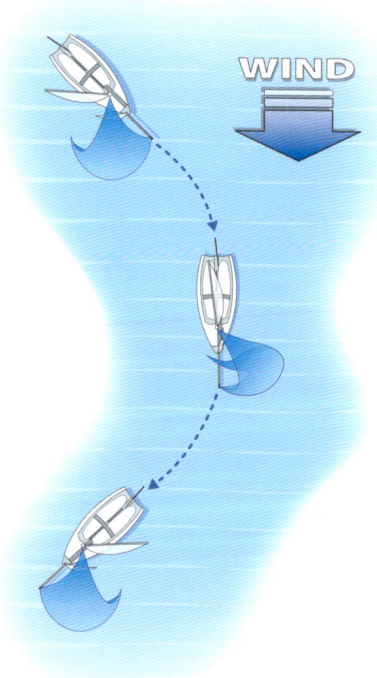

The speed with which you steer through the gybe must reflect the ability of the crew members to move across the boat. If the helm turns the boat at the right speed the negative forces on it won't create excessive heeling. Communication between helm and crew is vital as you move in a co-ordinated manoeuvre. Plan the manoeuvre together beforehand.

Helm

- Concentrate on steering.
- Greater speed into the gybe reduces the load on the rig, making gybing easier.

- As it gets windier, you will need a correction factor in the turn to send the boat back down onto a broad reach/run – the 'M' gybe.
- Judge this by mainsheet loads and help the boom across with your mainsheet hand.
- Let the mainsheet run out to allow the boom to go all the way to the shroud in higher winds. Use a knot in the mainsheet to control this.

Gybe

Immediate bear away

Head up into power zone

Crew

- Prepare the new spinnaker and jib sheet before the gybe by taking up the slack.
- As you ease your weight inboard in preparation for the gybe, keep setting the spinnaker (normally by easing the sheet).
- When the helm calls "Gybe-Ho", start to move across the boat and pull on the old sheet to flatten the spinnaker across the jib.
- As you move to the new side of the boat, pull on the new sheet and allow the old one to run free.
- As the spinnaker inflates on the new gybe, ease it until it is set with a small curl in the luff.
- Sit out harder or trapeze to set the course and balance.
- Set the jib.

TOP TIP

Aim to turn the boat so that both helm and crew can sit on the new windward-side deck. The stronger the wind, the smaller the angle you will turn through to gybe.

Dropping the Spinnaker

As many spinnaker chute systems will be rigged on the port side of the boat, dropping on port will involve pulling the spinnaker around the jib. It's better to drop on starboard if possible. If you have to drop on port, bear away onto a run which will take the sideways wind pressure off the spinnaker and allow an easier drop. A good indicator is if the luff of the sail has moved to windward of the bow.

Step 1:

Bear away to allow the crew to go into the boat. To control the spinnaker, the crew stands on the sheet or passes it to the helm. Take up the slack in the retrieval line to depower the spinnaker, then uncleat the halyard. If there is a separate pole outhaul, uncleat this too.

Step 2:

Pull as quickly as possible to prevent the spinnaker going in the water. The helm will need to steer carefully to keep the boat balanced; the trick is to steer to keep the hull directly under the mast.

Step 3:

On some boats, complete the drop by transferring from the retrieval line to the sail to pull it fully into the boat. Tidy up the sheets and recleat the halyard.

TOP TIP

Continuous rolling can be a problem downwind. On asymmetrics, check the centreboard is down. Crew and helm sit still and helm steers to counteract the roll.

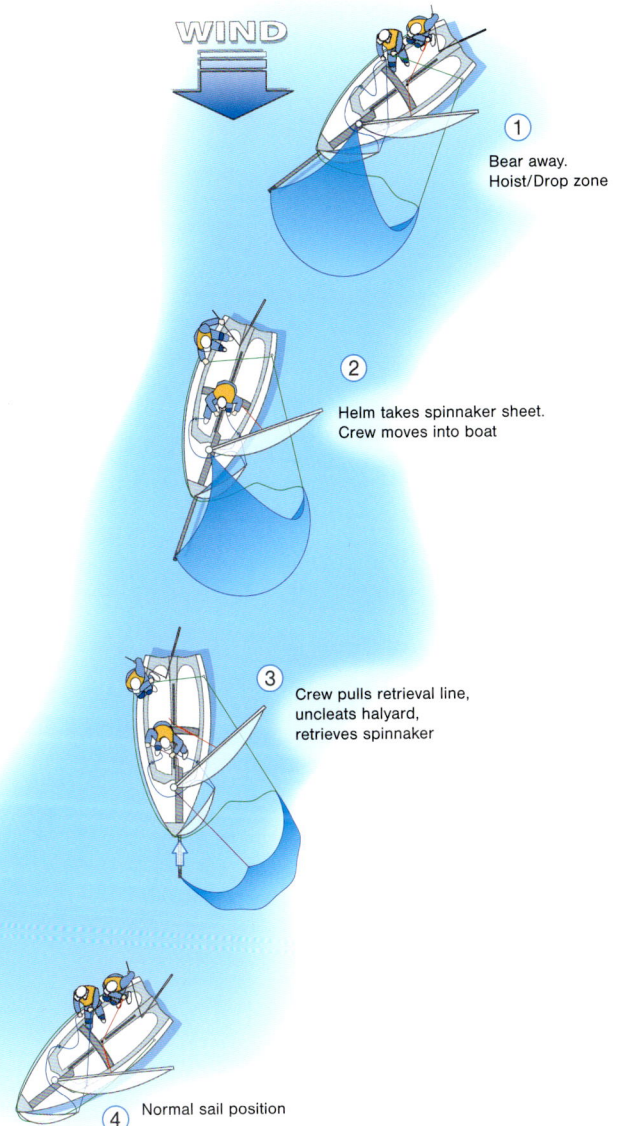

Symmetrical Spinnaker Handling

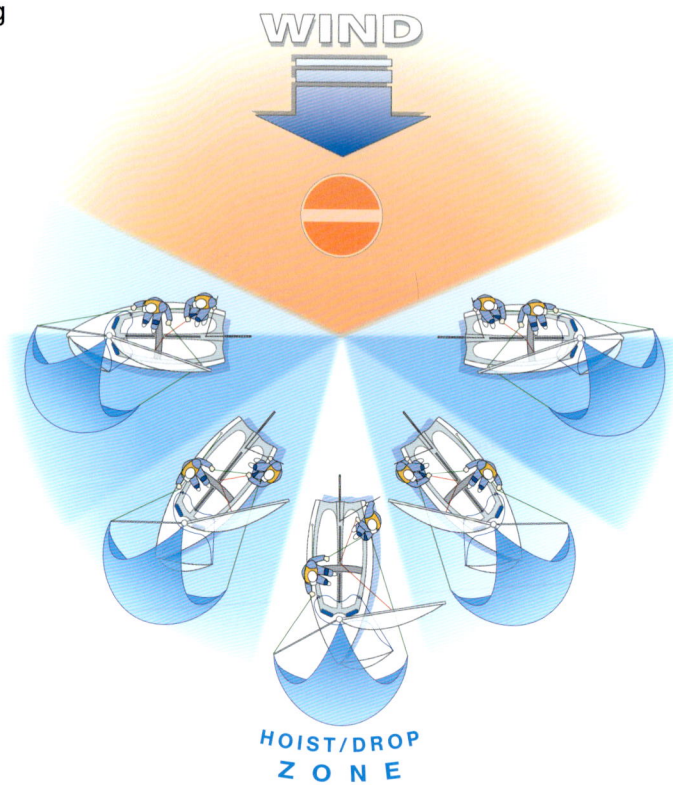

The symmetrical spinnaker is a little more complex to fly. This section primarily addresses launching from bags, as launching from a chute is easier and is treated as if it is a leeward launch from a bag.

Leeward Hoist/Chute Hoist:

The method is: POLE ON – HOIST – SET.

Step 1:

Attach the pole to the guy (hook facing up). Attach the uphaul/downhaul rope to the pole. Then attach the pole to the mast. The pole should hook onto the mast with the hook facing up, for easy retrieval.

Step 2:

Bear away so that the spinnaker can be hoisted. One crew member (usually the helm) hoists while the other (usually the crew) attends to the sheet and guy.

Step 3:

If you are on a broad reach or a reach, put the guy in a reaching hook or pull it down using a twinning line. This allows you to hike or trapeze and cuts down the stretch in the guy.

Step 4:

Once fully up, pull on the guy until the pole touches the clew of the spinnaker. Now pull back on the guy until the pole and clew of the spinnaker are at approximate right angles to the apparent wind. The pole height should allow the two clews to fly at the same height by adjusting the pole uphaul.

Downwind, the helm sits to leeward holding the boom and the crew sits to windward to allow them to view and set the spinnaker easily.

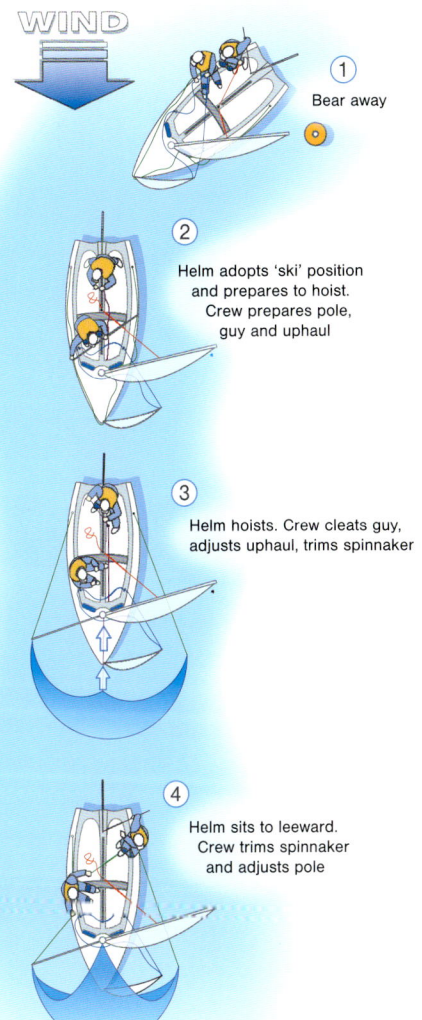

① Bear away

② Helm adopts 'ski' position and prepares to hoist. Crew prepares pole, guy and uphaul

③ Helm hoists. Crew cleats guy, adjusts uphaul, trims spinnaker

④ Helm sits to leeward. Crew trims spinnaker and adjusts pole

TOP TIP

To check pole height, ease the spinnaker sheet. The luff should fold in the middle and peel towards the head and foot. Peeling from the top or bottom indicates the pole is at the wrong height.

Windward Hoist

The method is: LAUNCH – POLE ON – SET.

Depending on the previous drop, the spinnaker may be in the windward bag. Throw the spinnaker around the forestay and jib before putting up the spinnaker pole.

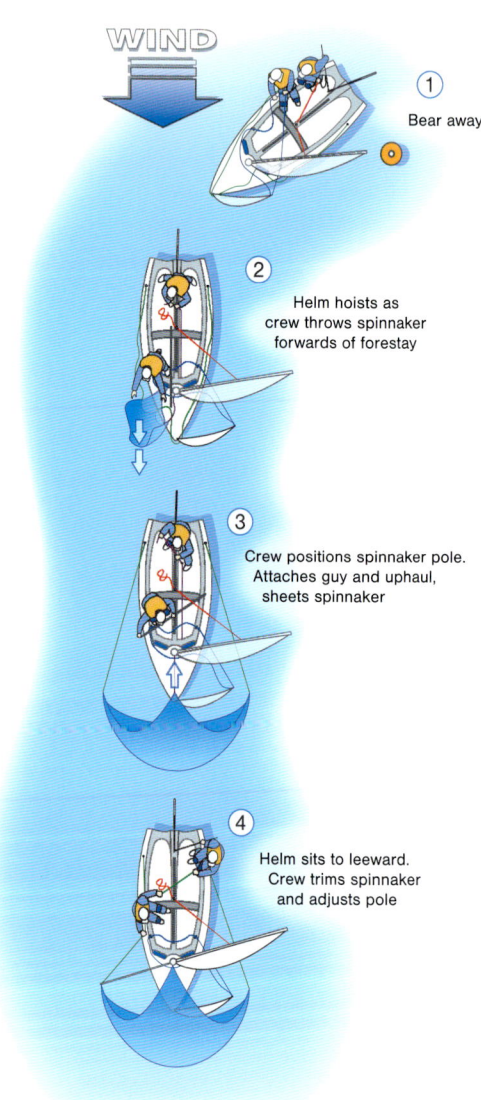

1. Crew gathers the spinnaker in their hands and, upon a call from the crew/helm, throws it forward and in front of the forestay. At the same time the helm hoists as quickly as possible.
2. The wind will blow the spinnaker to the new side.
3. The crew now attaches the spinnaker pole as before and sets the guy at the correct angle.

Trimming the Spinnaker

Trimming symmetric spinnakers is very similar to asymmetrics except that the pole angle must be correct, as on the previous pages. Sheet in until the luff of the sail is just curling. If the curl starts at the top or the bottom, re-adjust the pole height using the uphaul/downhaul.

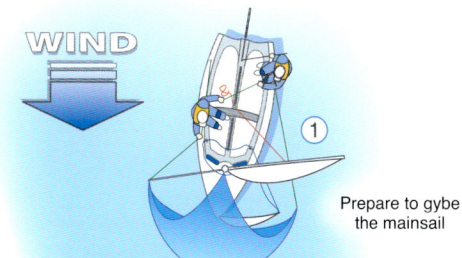

Gybing the Spinnaker

The sequence for gybing will vary, depending upon what type of twinning line/reaching hook you use.

- Hold down the twinning lines before the gybe to depower the spinnaker and give greater control.
- Release the lines after the gybe. Alternatively, the helm can choke the kite behind the mainsail by holding both the sheet and guy.

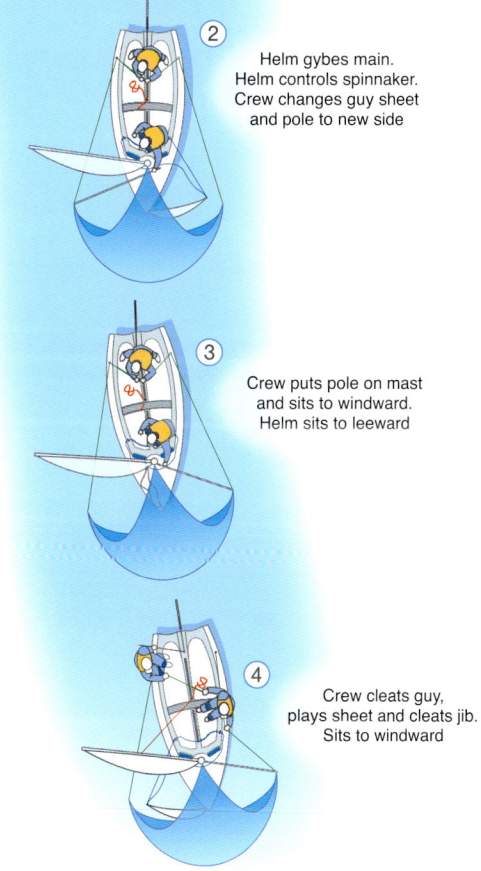

1. Prepare to gybe the mainsail

2. Helm gybes main. Helm controls spinnaker. Crew changes guy sheet and pole to new side

3. Crew puts pole on mast and sits to windward. Helm sits to leeward

4. Crew cleats guy, plays sheet and cleats jib. Sits to windward

There are numerous ways to gybe conventional spinnakers. The key is to have a system and stick to it, while playing to your strengths. If the helm is good at steering he or she may steer with the tiller between his or her legs and trim the guy and sheet during the gybe. Alternatively, the guy and sheet may be cleated off for the gybe. Whatever system you use, commitment, communication and speed are vital.

TOP TIP

Throw the spinnaker sharply forwards around the forestay.

Run-to-run Gybe

As with asymmetric spinnaker manoeuvres, steering is the key. Aim to follow the spinnaker round, while balancing the forces acting on the boat.

1. The crew rotates the spinnaker back towards the wind by pulling on the guy, while the helm initiates the gybe with a small amount of rudder movement. Gybe the mainsail first.
2. After the boom is across the boat, the spinnaker pole is transferred from the mast to the new guy. At this point, the pole may be on both the new guy and the old guy.
3. Release the pole from the old guy and attach it to the mast. Remember – hook facing up.
4. Place the new guy in the reaching hook/twinning line and carry on trimming as before. Gybing run-to-run is easier than reach-to-reach because the boat turns through a smaller angle. During a reach-to-reach gybe, pull the spinnaker much further round the forestay. In this type of gybe the sail may well collapse.

TOP TIP

If you struggle to remove the pole from the mast, ease the downhaul line a little before the gybe.

Dropping the Spinnaker into Bags

The spinnaker is best dropped on the windward side. If you are racing using bags, consider which gybe to drop from in order to then facilitate a leeward hoist at the next windward mark.

1. Remove the pole from the mast, guy and uphaul and stow.
2. Fly the kite until the correct distance from the mark.
3. Helm drops the spinnaker halyard while the crew pulls the leech down and into the windward bag. Ensure you are under the windward jib sheet.
4. The foot will lie on the foredeck until the entire spinnaker is stowed. Ensure all the spinnaker is in the bag.

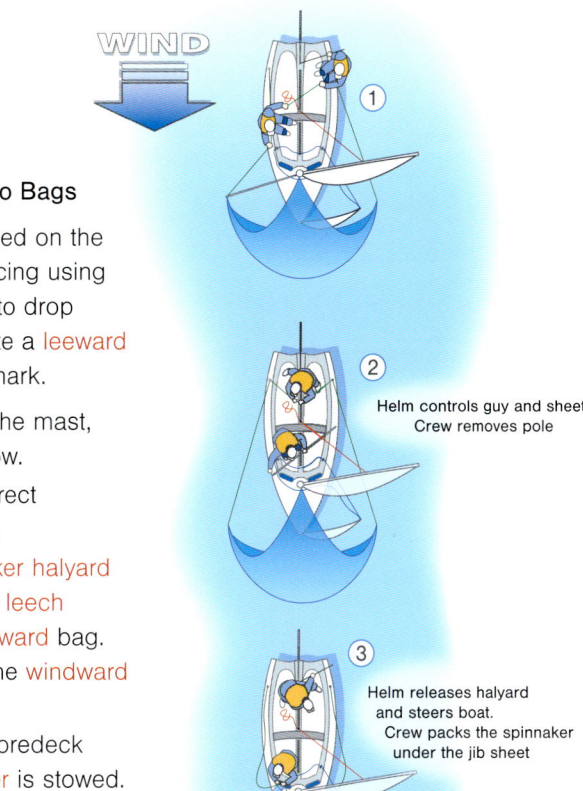

Helm controls guy and sheet.
Crew removes pole

Helm releases halyard and steers boat.
Crew packs the spinnaker under the jib sheet

For a chute drop, simply pull the spinnaker into the chute with the downhaul and then store the pole.

TOP TIP

Working down one leech stops twists. Always separate the two clews to reduce the chance of twists.

Apparent Wind

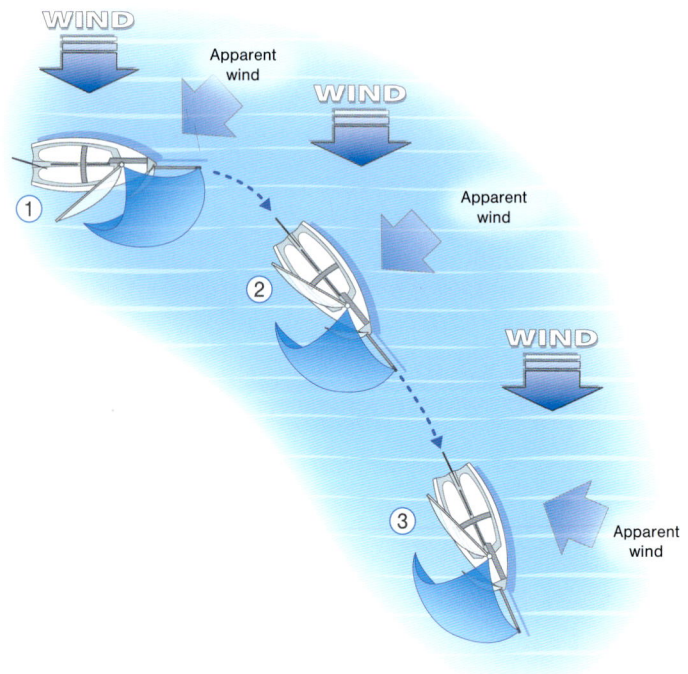

Apparent wind is the sailing domain of lightweight planing dinghies, catamarans and windsurfers. It is the combination of true wind (the wind you feel while stopped) and the wind created by your own speed. Remarkably, it has two significant advantages:

- It is shifted further forward than the true wind.
- It is stronger than the true wind.

When you bear away to handle stronger winds (2), you will have to bear away further still to allow for the apparent wind being forward (3). This double advantage enables very deep angles to be sailed on a windward/leeward course.

This is a relatively simplistic approach and you will need more detail as you gain experience.

Dinghies and Skiffs

Displacement dinghies and skiffs are at opposite ends of the scale. At one end, we have dinghies that will only plane in very strong winds. At the other, we have skiffs which plane upwind and downwind in light breezes.

The skiff is characterised by very light weight and significant righting ability via wings, trapeze or both. The skiff also has a very flat rocker (the amount of curvature in the length of the hull from bow to stern) that aids planing but hinders light-wind performance. In general, the skiff is better suited to the advanced sailor as it places a significant emphasis on technique. However, most skiff types have large rudder blades for easier control. Because they sail fast downwind, pressure on the rig is low and gybing is relatively easy.

TOP TIP

Losing control? Bear away into the safe zone to regain balance and reduce power.

5 TRAPEZING

In order to exert the maximum righting leverage, many boats are provided with racks, a trapeze wire, or both, to enable the crew to move further out. Trapezing is generally less tiring than hiking. Most trapeze boats are equipped with spinnakers. There are a few exceptions, including some multihulls.

Trapeze Harnesses

A good harness should fit snugly and offer minimal opportunities for snagging on rigging, etc. The hook should be positioned near your centre of gravity (facing down), and hooks into a ring suspended from the trapeze wire. The ring will be of adjustable height so that you can raise and lower yourself according to the amount of leverage required and whether you are positioned forward or back. Good non-slip footwear is essential.

Getting Out

The trapeze wire will always tend to pull you forwards, so lead with your front foot. In general, the front leg supports your weight and the back leg is used for balance. If necessary, lean towards the back of the boat a little.

1. Grab the handle with your front hand and hook on with your back hand.

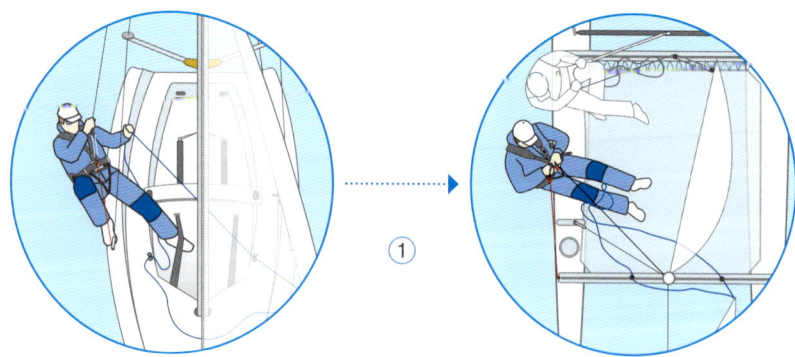

2. Take your weight on the trapeze wire and move out onto the side of the boat or rack, taking the jib or spinnaker sheet with you. Use your back hand for support if necessary but keep your weight on the trapeze ring.

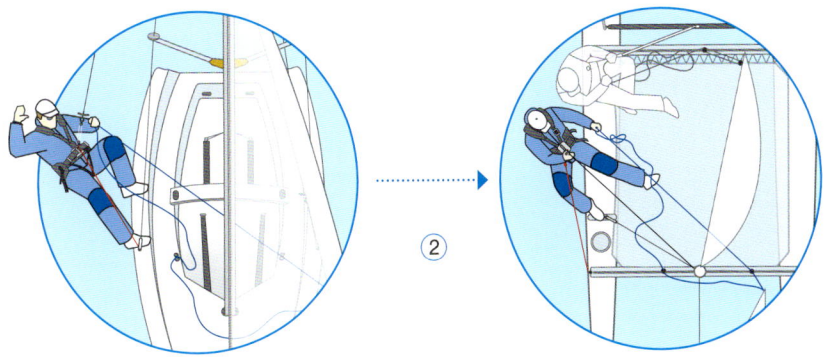

3. Step out of the boat, pushing on your front foot. Ease the jib sheet as you move out.

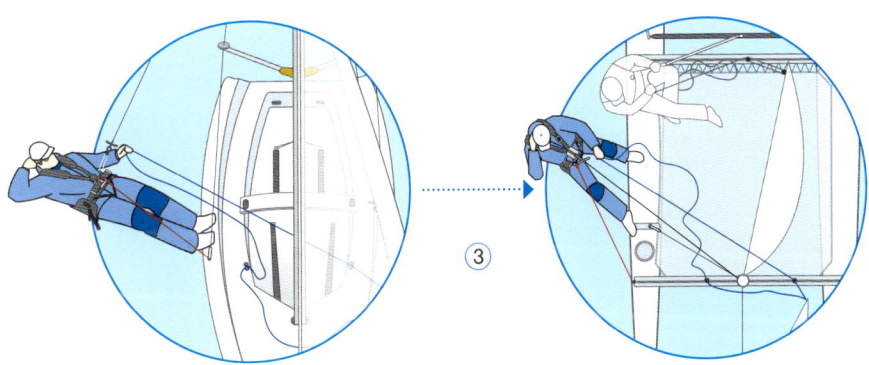

4. Follow with the back foot, and relax your shoulders into the harness. You can then release the handle with your rear hand. While you may find the sheet initially useful to keep your balance, try to be aware of your balance through your feet.

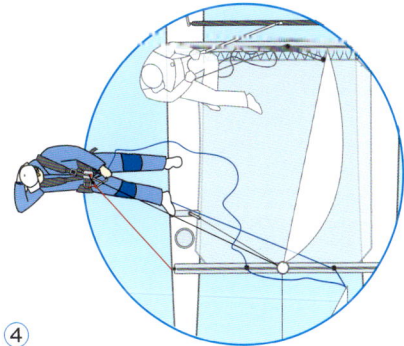

> **TOP TIP**
>
> Start with the trapeze ring high, an easier position. Lower yourself as you gain confidence.

On the Trapeze

Traditionally, the crew trapezes flat for maximum leverage. However, modern asymmetric boats have low freeboard, so a higher position is increasingly common. With your body at an angle it is easier to move in and out. This also ensures you are clear of waves and have better all-round visibility.

Teamwork is important and in gusty conditions the helm may move inboard to enable the crew to stay out. Equally, the crew may hold the helm's shoulder for stability in certain conditions. Sailing downwind you may need to move well back and lower yourself on the wire.

Getting In

To come off the trapeze, reverse the procedure for getting out. Bend the front leg, holding the sheet in your rear hand and using this hand for support. While in traditional boats you may unhook from the ring in a sitting position, most asymmetrics require that you stay on your feet as you tack or gybe the boat.

Capsizing from the Trapeze

If you capsize to leeward, try to lower yourself into the water, unhooking from the trapeze ring first. If you jump you may damage sails or rigging, or become entangled yourself. If you are quick you may manage to climb directly onto the centreboard. A windward capsize will be very wet. Your priority once capsized will be to unhook yourself quickly and move to the back of the boat, clear of the sails etc., as the boat settles on its side.

> **TOP TIP**
>
> Communication is crucial with the crew on the trapeze. Warn the crew before altering course and discuss how to share responsibilities; e.g. when under spinnaker, crew concentrates on trimming spinnaker and helm watches for gusts and traffic.

6 START RACING

There are hundreds of sailing clubs throughout the UK. They nearly all organise regular racing, along with training and social events.

Racing is organised all year round, with the clubs carrying on through the winter months usually only racing at weekends due to failing light. During the summer most clubs sail at weekends and on some weekday evenings.

Clubs provide storage space for dinghies and a regular meeting place for people with an interest in sailing.

If there are sufficient boats of the same class it is normal to organise a separate start. However, it is possible to run races together with many different types of dinghy using a handicap system called the RYA Portsmouth Yardstick Scheme.

The RYA Portsmouth Yardstick Scheme

The RYA Portsmouth Yardstick Scheme is a method of applying handicaps to sailing boats to allow different types of boat to compete on level terms.

It is based on the race results sent in by sailing clubs at the end of each year. From these, the Portsmouth Numbers can be worked out or updated. Essentially, each type of boat is allocated a Portsmouth Number (PN) roughly based around a thousand. The lower the number the faster the boat. If a boat with a PN of 950 takes 950 seconds to go around a course, a boat with a number of 1,050 should cover the same course in 1,050 seconds.

When Boats Meet

When boats are on opposite tacks, a port-tack boat shall keep clear of a starboard-tack boat.

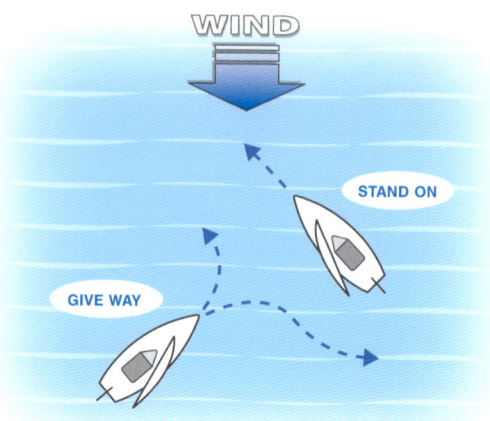

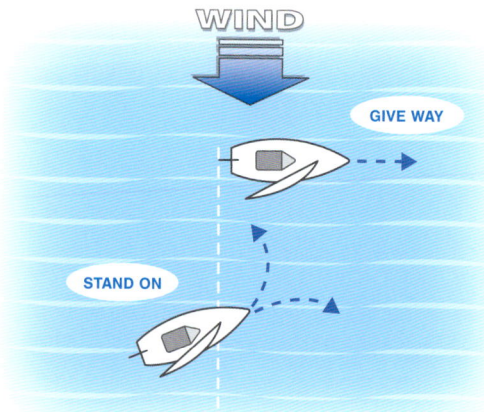

When boats are on the same tack and overlapped, a windward boat shall keep clear of a leeward boat.

When boats are on the same tack and not overlapped, a boat clear astern shall keep clear of a boat clear ahead.

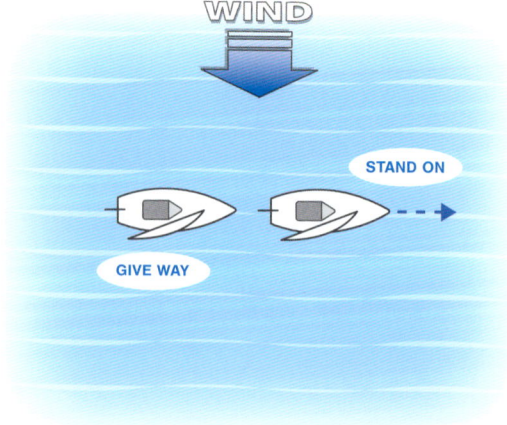

Starting a Race

A race is started with a countdown, leading to all the boats crossing an imaginary line usually from the downwind side and going towards a buoy somewhere upwind.

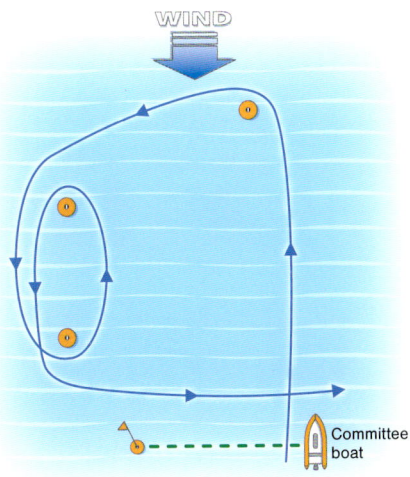

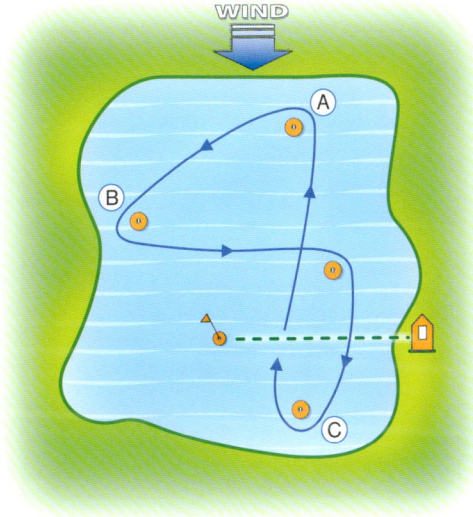

The start line is sighted between two points, either buoys, masts on boats, or markers on the land.

The aims of a good start are as follows:

- To cross the start line immediately after the start signal.
- To be travelling at full speed as soon as possible.
- To be able to go upwind by the best route, unhindered by other boats.
- To stay clear of other boats so they can't slow you down.
- To cross the start line at the most advantageous point.

Explanation of Signals

Individual Recall X

General Recall X

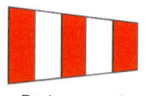
Postponement

Preparatory P

Disqualification Black Flag

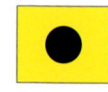
1 Minute Rule

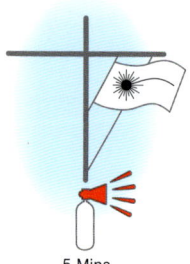
5 Mins

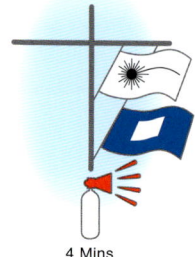
4 Mins

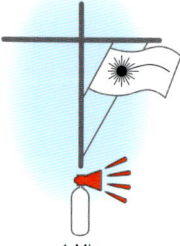
1 Min

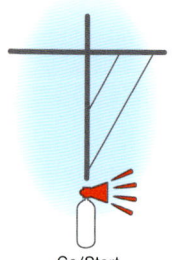
Go/Start

Unlike in athletics, a premature start does not necessarily result in a restarted race. Instead, the race officer will sound another signal and raise the 'X' flag. This informs the sailors that somebody jumped the start and they must turn around and recross the line.

However, if several boats start early the race officer will start the race again. He or she can, on subsequent starts, use different flags in place of the 'P' flag to signal different penalties to deter people from starting early.

For more information, refer to the rules book and your club sailing instructions.

TOP TIP

The sound signals are used to draw sailors' attention to the visual signals (the flags). Take your timing from the visual signals.

Where on the Starting Line?

Aim to start in clean air – as clear of other boats as possible.

One of the most important rules in sailing is the port/starboard rule. So as to try and prevent collisions, a boat on port tack must keep clear of a boat on starboard tack. Because the start inevitably has lots of boats going upwind, close to each other, it is generally easier to start on starboard tack.

A windward boat must keep clear of a leeward boat because it is farthest from the direction from which the wind is blowing. In the Square Line example, B and C must keep clear of A on the line.

Square Line

If the starting line is exactly at right angles to the wind, there is no advantage in starting at one end or the other. The distance to the windward mark will be the same and A, B and C start equally.

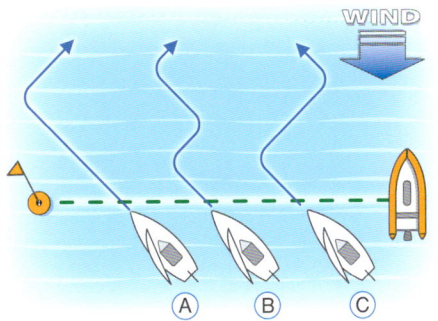

Room to Accelerate

Get the boat going as fast as you can as quickly as you can. It can take several seconds to accelerate a boat to full speed when going to windward. Sail faster as you approach the line by aiming 10 degrees or so off the wind, provided that you have room to leeward. A starts fastest.

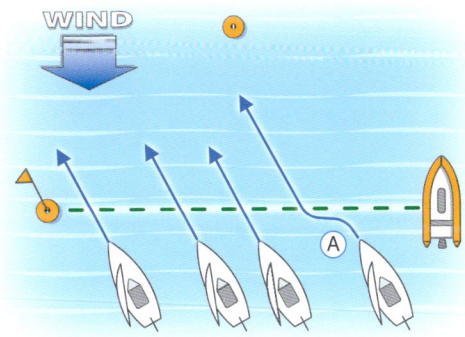

Bias

If the start line is not quite at right angles to the wind then one end of the starting line will be further upwind than the other and therefore nearer to the first buoy. The line is said to be biased. Sail along the line in both directions, with your mainsail right out. The end you can sail away from more easily is the one to start from. A leads B.

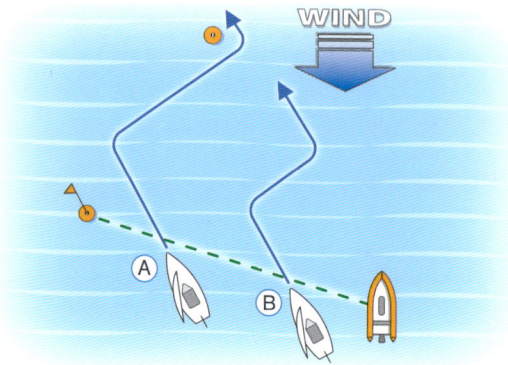

How Do I know When I'm on the Line?

It can be difficult to judge whether or not you are on the imaginary line, so it is worth taking a transit.

Sail beyond the start line, sight along it and find an object on shore that is on the line.

You can now tell if you are up to the start line (or not) by sighting the end of the line with the object beyond it. Be aware that quite a lot of the boat protrudes in front of you. A reads the transits and starts on time.

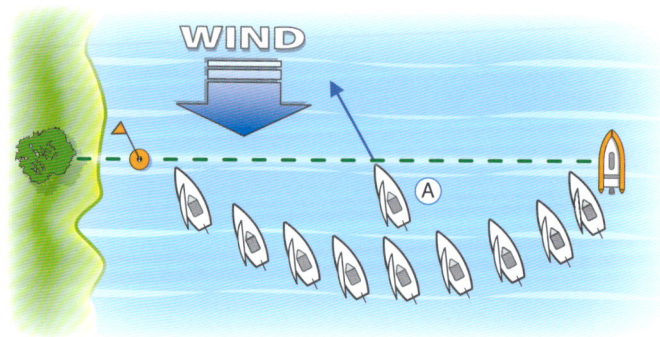

Going up the Beat

Making Best use of the Breeze

Because the wind rarely comes from a consistent direction for very long, big advantages can be achieved by being on the tack that takes you nearest to the windward mark. Changes in wind direction tend to occur during gusts and lulls, and keen-eyed sailors will see their effect on the water before they arrive. With good communication between the helm and crew you can be ready to tack if the wind heads you (takes you further away from the windward buoy) or turn upwind a little if the wind lifts you (takes you nearer the windward buoy).

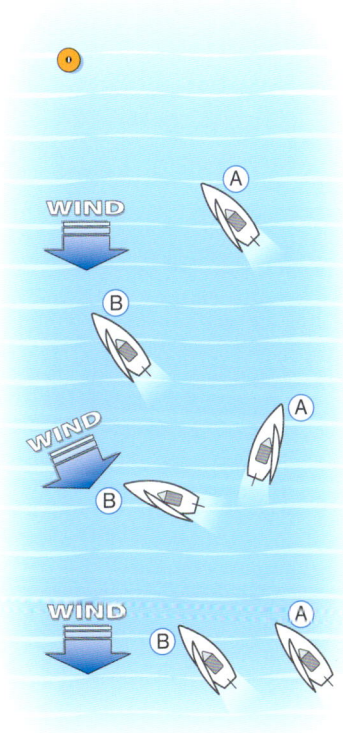

A notices the header and tacks, then tacks again when the wind oscillates back. A is ahead of B.

The boat should be sailed as fast as possible (see chapter 7, Performance Sailing). Generally, the boat should be level (balanced) with the sails in tight and the controls adjusted to suit the wind strength. Use the 5 Essentials.

Which Side of the Beat?

You can make gains upwind by traveling up the most advantageous side of the beat. As you tack going up the beat you travel to the left- and the right-hand side of a straight line to the windward buoy. Very often the wind or the water flow on one side will be more advantageous than on the other.

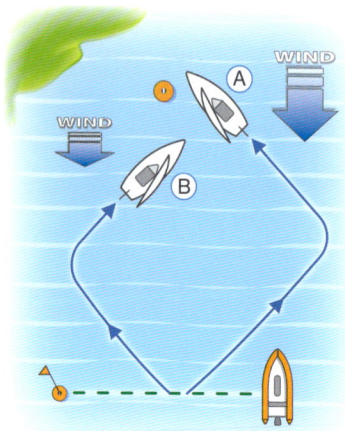

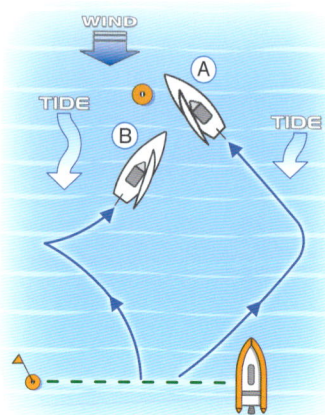

Tacking for the Mark

A lay line is the imaginary line that extends down from the windward buoy depicting a windward course to it. Tack to get to the windward buoy as soon as possible. C travels further, tacks late and falls behind A and B.

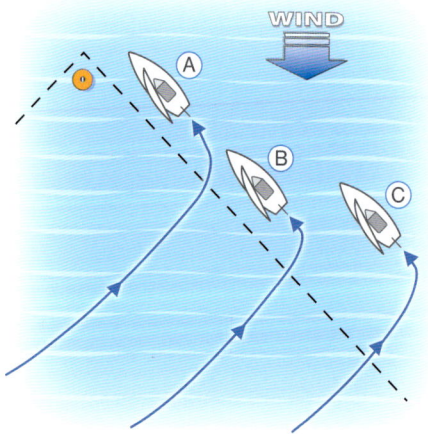

TOP TIP

Extra effort in the first 60 seconds after the start can put you in clean air and allow you to tack without other boats in the way.

At the Windward Mark

Tactics

- Approach on starboard tack if possible to gain right of way over boats on port tack.
- Locate the next buoy before you get to the windward buoy so you are ready to turn straight onto the new course.
- Ease the kicking strap before and raise the centreboard after you turn (depending on boat type and course).
- Keep the boat flat or heel to windward as you bear away around the buoy. This will make the boat want to turn downwind.
- Ensure the boom is clear of the buoy as you let the sail out.
- Be aware of other boats around you.
- Communication between helm and crew is vital.

Three-boat-length Circle

Many rules refer to the three-boat-length circle. This is simply an imaginary circle around the buoy with a radius of three boat lengths.

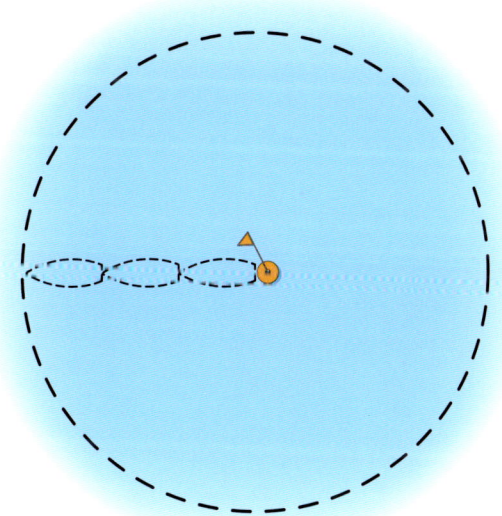

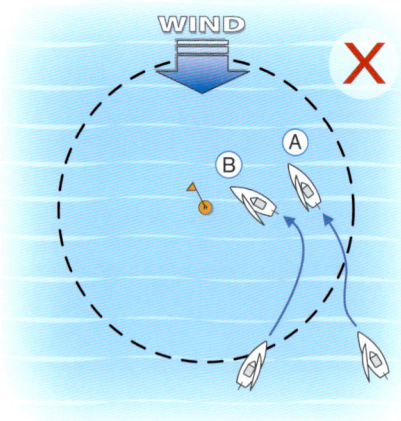

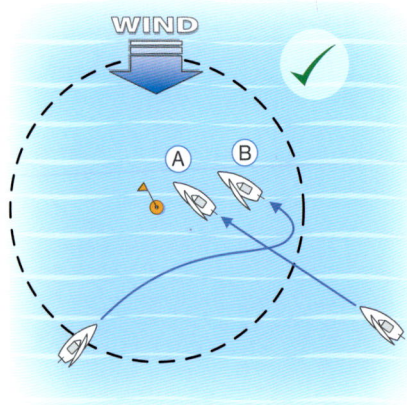

Three Boat Lengths at Windward Mark

Most windward buoys are left to port, so it is advantageous to approach the buoy on starboard tack. Some boats will come towards the buoy on port tack and have to tack before going round the buoy. There is a rule to reduce the risk of collisions that restricts what these boats may do.

No boat approaching on port and tacking inside the three-boat-length circle may cause a boat on starboard to have to luff (turn upwind) beyond a close-hauled course. Any boat doing so must take a penalty. If there are lots of boats on starboard tack coming towards the buoy it is safer for a port-tack boat to tack outside the three-boat-length circle.

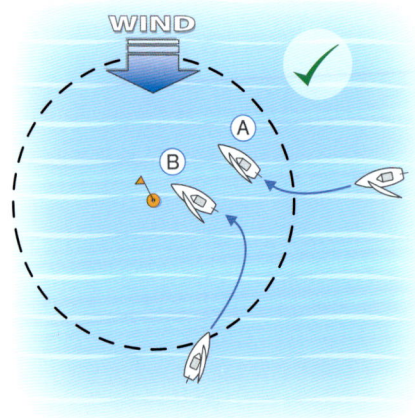

Reaching and Running

While you may steer straight between the off-wind marks, try to stay in the strongest wind by sailing low in the gusts and high in lighter breeze.

Luffing Rights

You may wish to stop a boat overtaking to windward. To do this you may luff above your course to the next buoy, but the overtaking boat must have time to respond. You may not luff beyond head to wind. The overtaking boat must keep clear to windward of you unless it gets clear ahead. If it does you must immediately return to your original course.

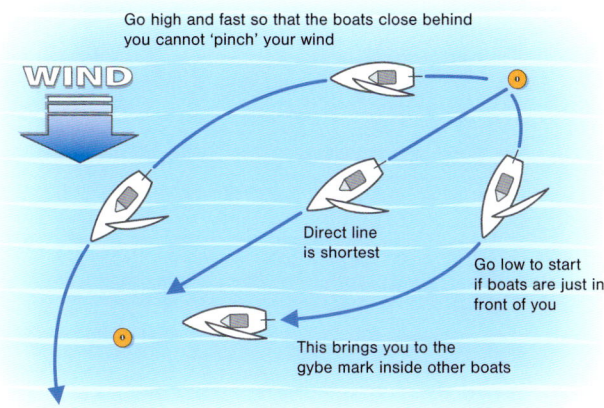

Don't luff unless you're sure it's worth the lost time – this tactic often costs places in the race.

TOP TIP

To decide if you are in another boat's dirty wind, look to see if their burgee is pointing at you. If it is then you are probably being slowed down.

Running

When running straight downwind, be aware of boats behind you. Because the wind reaches them first, it is disturbed and slower by the time it reaches you, resulting in the boats behind catching you up. It is therefore better to try and sail on one side of the boats behind you.

At an Off-wind Mark

Three Boat Lengths at an Off-wind Mark

When arriving at an off-wind buoy close to another boat, the racing rules dictate whether you are entitled to pass between the other boat and the buoy.

When the first boat enters the three-boat-length circle, the inner boat is only entitled to room if there is an overlap (1). If so, the outer boat must allow sufficient room for the inner boat to pass, allowing for a gybe if necessary. If there is no overlap, at the moment the first boat enters the circle the inner boat must go round the buoy behind the outer boat (2).

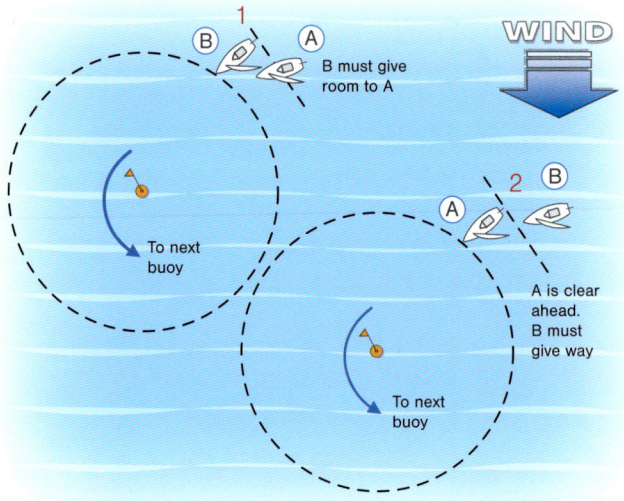

TOP TIP

A little water in the boat can slow it significantly. If the crew is not hiking or trapezing, the reach or run can be a good time to empty the boat.

Leeward Buoy, Last Beat and Finish

Wide in, Tight out

When passing the leeward buoy, aim to sail as close to it as possible as you start the beat. You should only turn as fast as you can sheet in.

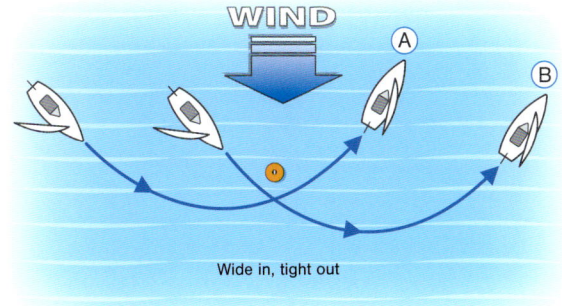

Wide in, tight out

Go in wide – a wide approach will enable you to sail very close to the mark as you leave upwind. To help the boat luff up, a small amount of leeward heel is useful.

A overtakes B.

TOP TIP

As you arrive at the leeward buoy, work out if there is any flow of water with you or against you. If it is against you, leave the boat setup for going downwind, including the spinnaker, until the last possible moment. If it is with you, drop early and set up for the beat to windward before rounding.

Last Beat, Consolidate and Cover

By the time you reach the last beat, the boats will probably be spread out.

The priority is to consolidate your position by not letting any boats past you. To reduce the chance of this happening, stay between the boats behind you and the finish line to ensure they don't receive any beneficial wind changes that you miss (loose covering).

If there is a boat near, try to stay directly upwind, keeping the boat in your dirty wind. A covers B (tight covering).

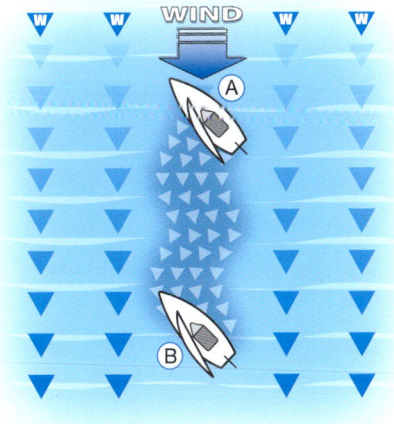

Finish Line

One end of the finish line may be to leeward of the other. Try and judge this and go for the end that is nearest to you – the downwind end. If you go beyond the lay line for the finish and there are other boats around you, you are allowed to hail for room to cross the finish line.

A is given room despite being the windward boat.

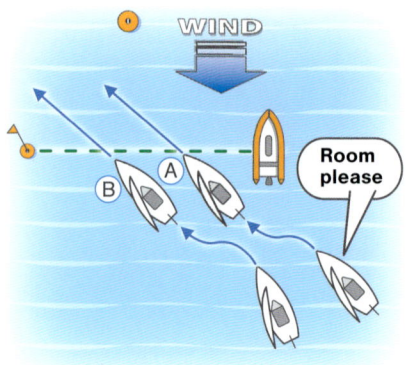

Wind Shifts

The wind is rarely steady, constantly changing in strength and direction. Studying the wind is a life-long pursuit. Aim to be in the best position, sailing as fast as possible. The wind gives you the opportunity to do both these things, so understanding and observation will be key. When sailing downwind, gusts give more speed and a lower course. Sailing upwind, gusts can be an advantage to increase speed, but more importantly shifts allow the greatest gain. In order to position yourself correctly you must differentiate between an oscillating shift and a persistent shift.

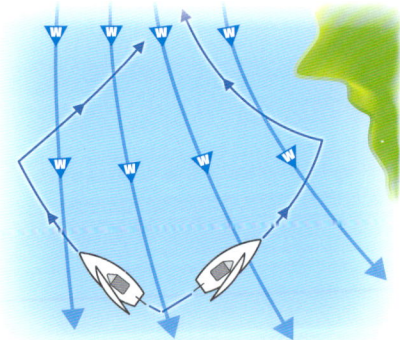

An oscillating shift moves in a series of shifts about a mean direction, while a persistent shift (such as a sea breeze) moves in one general direction (although it may oscillate as it goes in this direction). For the persistent shift, one side of the course will give a gain over the other side.

For oscillating shifts, sailors who tack onto the favoured lifted shift every time will make a gain. It is important to identify whether a shift is oscillating or persistent, as they each require a different reaction.

If you are lifted in an oscillating shift, stay on that tack as you are lifted. If you are lifted in a persistent shift, you will probably need to tack as the strategy will be to get to the inside of the bend. In order to do this, the earlier you take the headed course the quicker you will get the gain from the long-term lift. Sail on in a lift, but tack on a header.

> **TOP TIP**
>
> If racing, remember you have to go around marks. Tacking on every shift may not allow us to arrive at the mark.

> **TOP TIP**
>
> In light winds, sail in the strongest breeze regardless of direction. In medium and strong winds, go for wind direction, not strength.

Why do we need the Rules?

The rules allow fair racing and should prevent collisions. The majority of situations are covered by just a few rules. It is not necessary to understand them all when you start racing. A better understanding will come with experience. Be aware of your rights and obligations to others.

Penalties

Having broken a rule you can exonerate yourself by doing a penalty turn at the first opportunity. A penalty turn will normally be one turn or two turns as defined by the rules. A one-turn penalty is a tack and a gybe in the same continuous direction. A two-turn penalty is two tacks and two gybes taken continuously in the same direction. Find out what penalties are in place before you race.

Protests

If somebody breaks a rule but does not do their penalty turns then you may protest. Inform the other boat that you intend to protest by calling "Protest". If they still do not take a penalty you should inform the race officer of your protest at the end of the race and complete a protest form. In order to help in the resolution of rules disputes in a more immediate, accessible and appropriate way, the RYA Racing Charter encourages the use of advisory hearings (no penalty) or RYA arbitration (reduced penalty) as an alternative to a formal protest hearing where possible disqualification may be the outcome.

Boat Preparation for Racing

You do not need a brand-new boat and sails to do well, but some simple preparation will help:

- Make sure your boat is clean and free from any big scratches and dents in the water area.
- Check that all the controls work.
- Ensure the mast is in the same place, and at the same angle, as the fast boats in your class – check the tuning guide on the class website and talk to class sailors.
- Make sure the dinghy is as light as possible. Most classes have a minimum weight.
- Ensure your foils and spars are maintained.

Choosing a Boat

When you start racing, consider what the right boat is for you. You should consider:

- How big you are, your weight and height.
- What sort of water you will be sailing on (inland/coastal).
- What dinghies are already sailed there.
- How experienced you are.
- How difficult the dinghy is to sail.
- Whether to sail on your own or with a crew.

Insurance, Certificates, Memberships

Before you start racing you will need third-party insurance cover for your dinghy.

Many classes require a measurement certificate. This means that the boat has been measured, weighed and possibly buoyancy-tested to conform to class rules.

It is also a good idea to join your class association. They are a good source of information and organise class events and training days. The class website is an excellent place to start.

7 PERFORMANCE SAILING

In order to understand the forces on a boat, practise experimenting with them. Rudderless sailing is one of the best exercises in assisting you to understand this, but make sure you practice with lots of room around you! See page 30 in chapter 1 (Seamanship Skills) of this book.

Once you have mastered sailing on a beam reach, try sailing around a triangular course using all the points of sailing. This chapter is about understanding the forces on the boat – how to use them in light winds and neutralise them in strong winds.

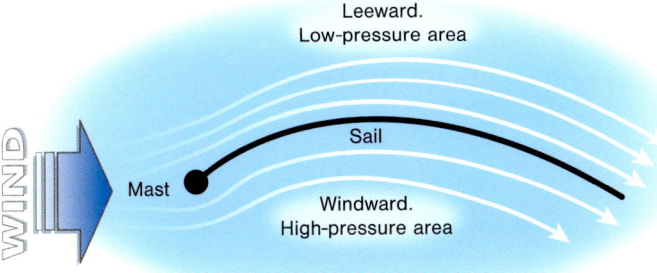

When air flows around a sail. The air travelling around the outside (leeward side) of the sail moves faster round the sail than the air on the windward side. This causes a difference in pressure on the two sides of the sail which pulls it to leeward. The force created by the sail acts roughly at right angles to the boom but only part of it drives the boat forward – the rest tries to push it sideways.

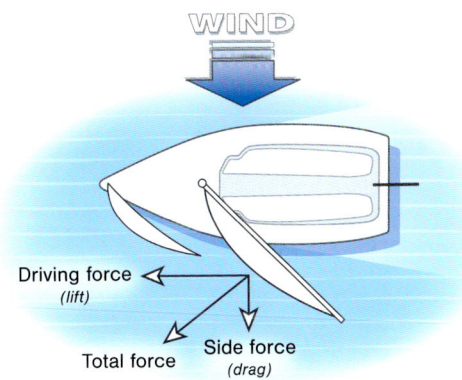

RYA Advanced Sailing 105

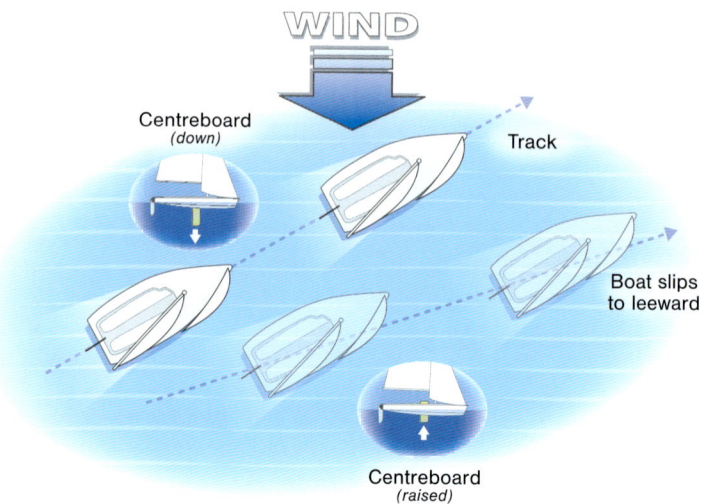

TOP TIP

When sailing without using the rudder, raise the centreboard by one-third. This reduces the heeling and turning forces by raising the centre of lateral resistance and moving it back.

How Keels, Centreboards and Daggerboards Work

A boat's keel, centreboard, or daggerboard is designed to resist the sideways force created by the sails. The rudder also plays a part. When the boat starts to move, water flows across the centreboard in much the same way as air flows across the sail. It creates a sideways force to windward that resists the opposite force on the sail. The two sideways forces cancel each other out, leaving a forward force which drives the boat. The force on the sails acts roughly at right angles to the boom. With sails in tight (when sailing close to the wind) the force acts mainly in a sideways direction. More sideways resistance is therefore required from the daggerboard. This is why most dinghies and some multihulls have a lifting centreboard or daggerboard, so that the area under the boat can be adjusted to suit the point of sailing.

Sailing Upwind

Tell Tales

The sails are sheeted in when sailing upwind. There are two basic ways to understand your performance. There is mechanical feedback from items such as tell tales, compass, burgees, and the luff (front) of the sail. There is also a more intuitive response, where you sense the 'feel' of the boat. The best option is to combine the two. The 'feel' will come with experience.

When sailing upwind, there are a number of variables:

- Wind direction.
- Balance (your ability to hike or trapeze).
- Steering a course.
- Sail setting (which will be fairly static).
- Centreboard, which will be fully down.
- Trim (which will be forward to stop transom drag).
- Created apparent wind due to speed (catamarans/skiffs).

TOP TIP

Always focus on the windward tell tales when sailing to windward.

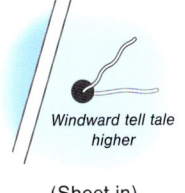

When learning, the tell tales are very important to give you feedback on steering. Keep looking to see how high you are pointing by luffing the boat slightly and checking the tell tales. At the perfect angle to the wind, the windward tell tales will stream slightly upwards.

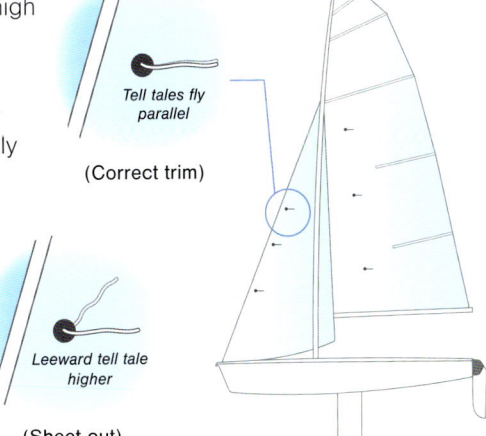

Intuition

In certain conditions, i.e. with wet tell tales sticking to the sail, feedback may be poor or non-existent, so try to develop an intuitive feel:

- Sail with your eyes shut for short periods.
- Look out for gusts, indicated for example by dark patches on water.
- Play with the sail controls and get feedback from your crew on how your steering is affected.

> **TOP TIP**
>
> Coat your tell tales with waterproofing (beeswax or lube spray) to reduce waterlogging.

Once you are fully hiked (and balanced), only steering and sail-setting will vary. If the jib is cleated in its correct beating position for the wind strength, the only variables will be the steering and the mainsheet. The helm must concentrate fully on steering while the crew looks for gusts, wind shifts and traffic. See page 66 in chapter 4, Sailing with Spinnakers, on holding the tiller extension and steering.

If you wander away from the wind, the sails will generate more sideways power than if fully close-hauled. This will result in having to ease the mainsheet to lose power. Instead, concentrate on pointing as close to the wind as possible (use the tell tales) and you will be able to handle the power without playing the mainsheet as much. This is called 'pinching' and ensures you are pointing more effectively.

> **GOLDEN RULE**
>
> Specific setup varies from class to class, so consult your class association. It does make a massive difference. Mast rake (forward and backward positioning) is used as the primary means of powering-up or depowering most dinghy and catamaran rigs.

Sailing Downwind – Reaching and Running

When using tell tales on the jib reaching downwind, sheet the sail until the windward tell tale collapses. Now ease until the leeward tell tale collapses. This will give you an idea of the sheeting 'band', within which you need to operate. Note that the upper tell tales will collapse first. As on a reach, exert a downward pressure on the sheet to control the leech. The jib cars can therefore be moved forward or out.

When running exactly downwind without a spinnaker, it normally pays to sheet the jib on the opposite side to the mainsail. This prevents it being blanketed by the mainsail and is known as goose-winging. Tell tales are not particularly helpful while running. You can also use a 'whisker pole' to hold out the jib on the opposite side to the main.

> **TOP TIP**
>
> If in doubt, always check the wind position by steering into the wind.

Rig Controls

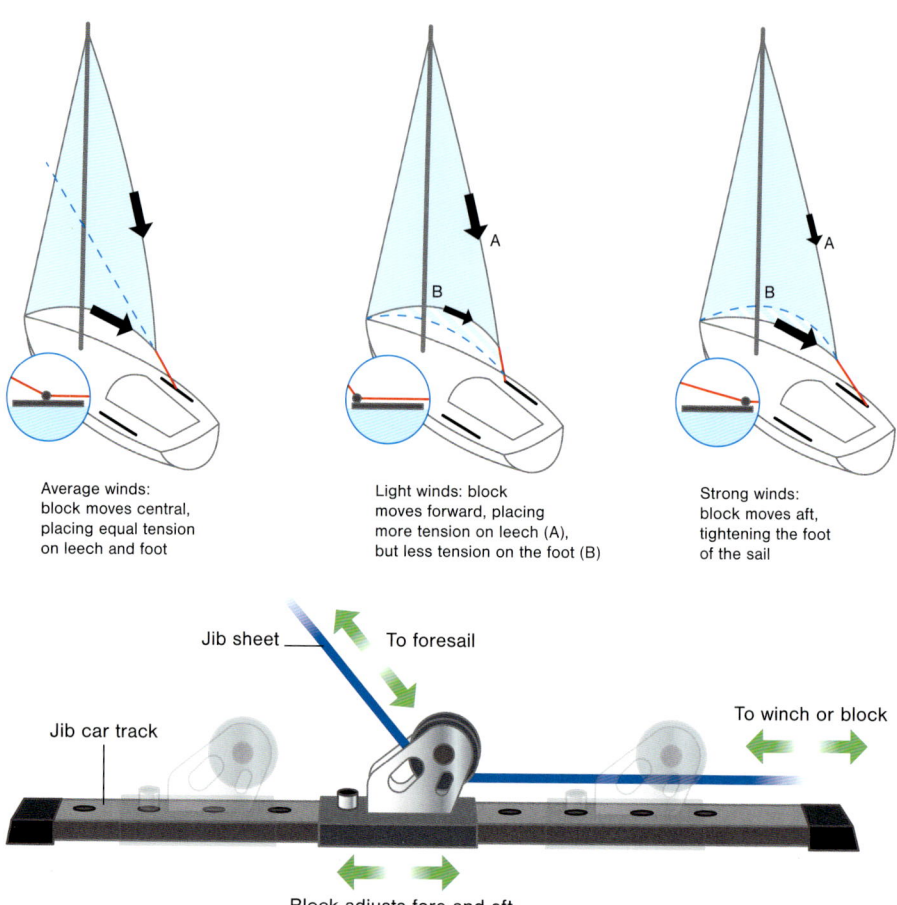

Average winds: block moves central, placing equal tension on leech and foot

Light winds: block moves forward, placing more tension on leech (A), but less tension on the foot (B)

Strong winds: block moves aft, tightening the foot of the sail

Block adjusts fore and aft

- The sheet varies the angle of the sail to the wind. In light winds, it tensions the jib leech according to the jib car position on the track.
- The kicker maintains mainsail twist, bends the mast and tensions the leech. Excessive amounts of kicker flatten the sail.
- The Cunningham compresses the mast, moves power forward in the mainsail and opens (eases) the leech.
- The outhaul flattens the lower part of the mainsail.

On catamarans, the mainsail downhaul replaces the Cunningham. Mainsail shape, mast bend and rotation, and leech tension are all controlled by mainsheet tension and traveller position.

Speed and Boat Handling

Light Winds

If you are sailing a two-person boat, the light-wind band varies from drifting conditions, where the crew sits to leeward, through to the crew being on the windward side but not hiking. In this wind band, which will vary according to your boat, concentrate on low drag, twisted sails and smooth movement with an emphasis on trim.

To check the trim, simply look at the transom drag. If it looks turbulent (A), move forward. This is particularly important in the new designs with very flat rockers.

Balance the boat with a small amount of leeward heel. This gives the rudder 'feel' – the boat tries to turn into the wind and will help the sails to set better. Too much rudder to correct this weather helm will cause turbulence and slow the boat down (B). The rudder will then act as a brake trying to resist the turning moment. You may have more control holding the tiller pan-handle style.

1. Boat heeled to leeward (balance).
2. Weight right forward (trim), transom clear of water.
3. Centreboard down.
4. Mast upright for maximum power.
5. Kicker slack, sail twisted to set for stronger breeze higher up.
6. No Cunningham – creases left in sail.
7. Outhaul light.
8. Sail flat to increase airflow.
9. Leech tell tales streaming.
10. Windward jib tell tales just lifting with jib cars back.

> **TOP TIP**
>
> Sheet in to point higher. If you over-sheet, the sail will stall, resulting in poor pointing and speed. If in doubt, ease the sheet.

Roll Tacks

In light winds, try to take advantage of gusts and wind shifts. You may find yourself tacking more often, which slows the boat, so use roll tacks. In roll tacking, the crew weight and the forces on the boat are used to your advantage, resulting in more efficient performance. The rudder resistance is reduced as the rudder is being used less to turn the boat. Roll tacks reduce the drag and deceleration as the boat turns upright and the sails flap, generating air resistance.

By rolling the boat with your body weight, the sails are fanned through the air, keeping them full for longer and dragging less. In this way the airflow is reattached to the sail quicker after the tack.

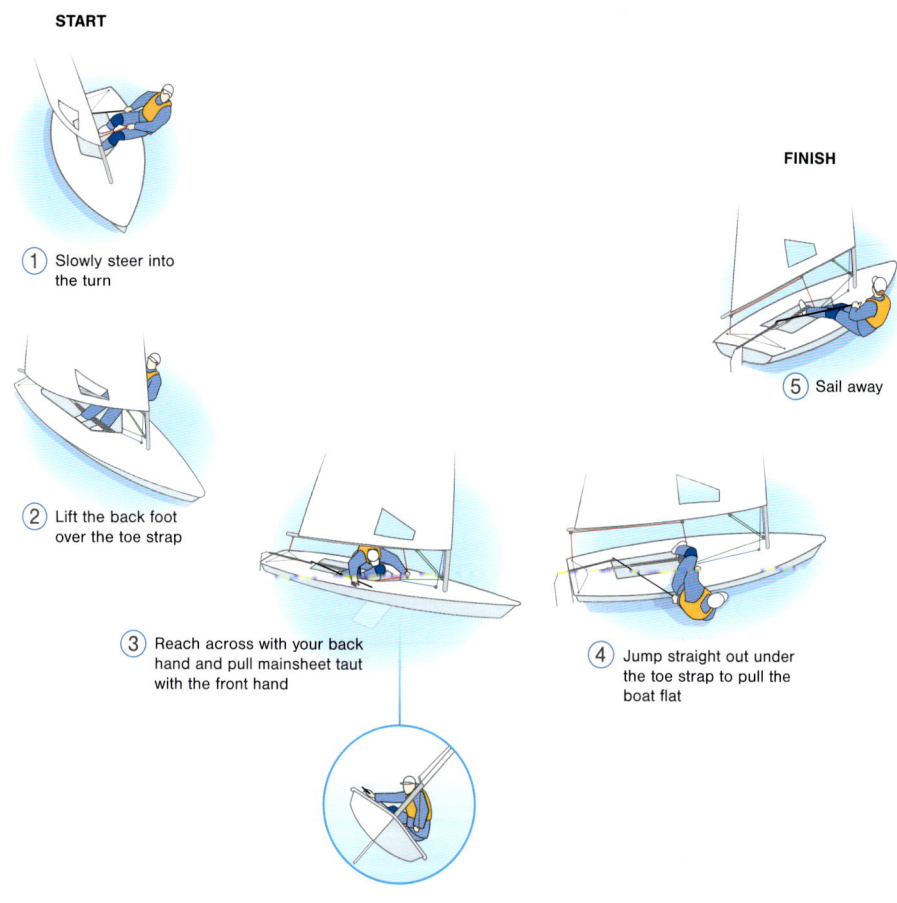

START

1. Slowly steer into the turn
2. Lift the back foot over the toe strap
3. Reach across with your back hand and pull mainsheet taut with the front hand
4. Jump straight out under the toe strap to pull the boat flat
5. Sail away

FINISH

Step 1:

Check the area is clear. Gently steer the boat head to wind by allowing the forces created by the leeward heel and a slight tiller angle to turn the boat. The crew joins the helm on the windward side to flick the mast and sails past head to wind.

Step 2:

As the sails collapse, cross the boat, sheet the jib across and ease the main a little. The forces on the rig help swing the bow away from the wind and onto the new close-hauled course.

Step 3:

The boat is pointing in the correct direction and will have excess leeward heel.

Step 4:

The helm and possibly the crew now move smoothly to windward while pulling in the sails, thus accelerating the boat back to its entry speed (in racing, going more than entry speed is illegal). The crew may now need to return to their leeward position to balance the boat.

Step 5:

Sail away.

The effectiveness of roll tacking will vary from boat to boat. The Enterprise is a near perfect roll tacking design. Roll tacking is not quite so effective with catamarans but, by moving crew weight to the windward quarter (the back corner) and spinning the boat on the inside hull as you enter the no-go zone, the boat will tack more effectively.

TOP TIP

If your roll tacks are too flat, delay the crew moving across the boat to join the helm by a second. You will only generate maximum roll past head to wind.

Roll Gybes

The same forces can be used to gybe the boat, with windward heel initiating the turn. Allow the mainsail to move across the boat by gentle assistance in its natural progress as, again, the forces on the boat and sails will be neutral. Smooth movement is the key. This manoeuvre can be used on dinghies, single-handers or with spinnakers.

Roll tacks and gybes can be used as the wind strength increases until you think that the forces are becoming too great to control. For example, you may have problems pulling the boat up again, having rolled the boat into the tack or gybe, so reduce the heel until you are tacking or gybing perfectly flat in strong winds.

Step 1:
Preparation: check the area is clear and the boom is clear of the shroud.

Step 2:
Roll the boat to windward to assist bearing away, mainsheet hand grasping the falls directly off the boom.

Step 3:
Gybe the main positively as the leech starts to lift. Centralise the tiller if necessary and cross the boat smartly to balance.

Step 4:
Balance the boat, sheet sails correctly and keep a good lookout.

TOP TIP

Footwork is crucial when tacking or gybing. Move your feet across the boat only when you yourself have to move across. Premature footwork can cause capsizes.

Many people gybe by standing up and pulling the tiller to windward, crossing the boat and centralising the tiller as the sail comes over. Skiff-style boats are better handled by continuously adjusting the tiller as the boat turns, only making a large tiller adjustment if balance becomes a problem.

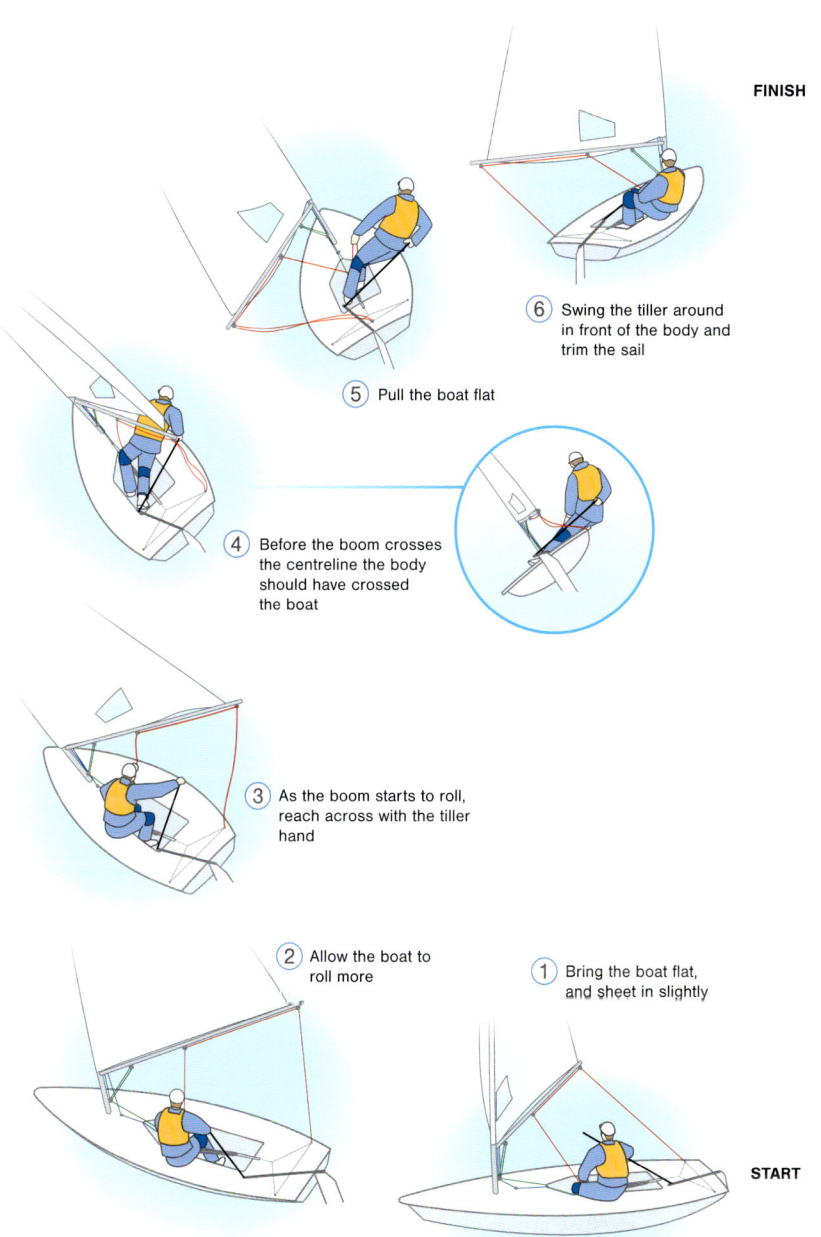

Light to Medium Winds

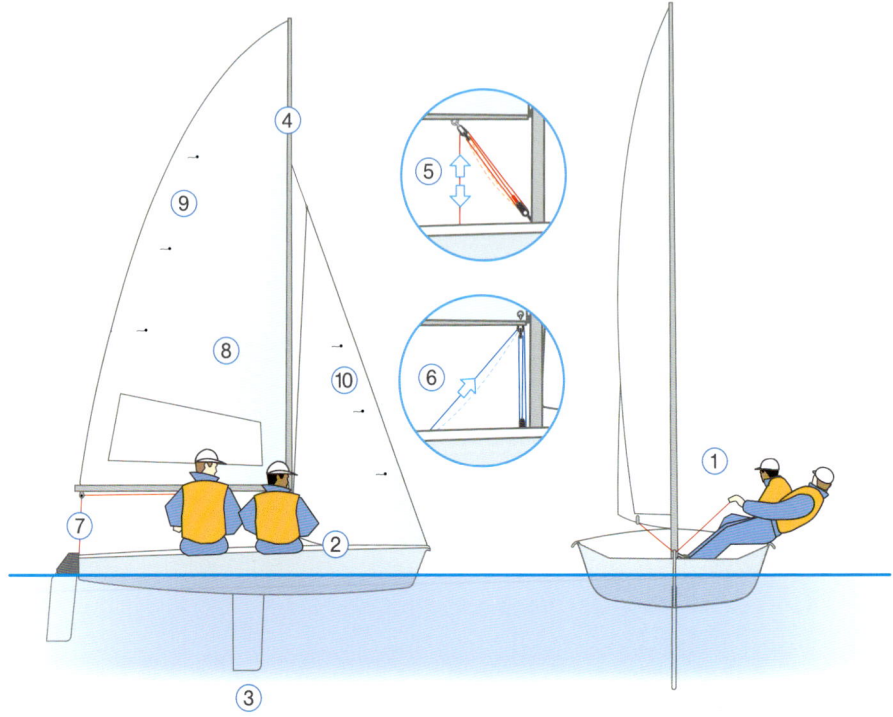

1. Boat level (balance), crew fully hiked.
2. Weight forward (trim).
3. Centreboard down.
4. Mast straight for maximum power, rake basically upright – see class tuning guide.
5. Take slack out of kicker, no tension. Small amount of mainsail twist.
6. No Cunningham – creases remain in sail.
7. Outhaul eased for maximum power.
8. Sail full for maximum power.
9. In general, leech tell tales just streaming.
10. Windward jib tell tales just lifting with jib cars forward a little.

In lighter winds, start with the crew sitting on the windward side but not hiking and end with the crew fully hiked and the rig at maximum power.

In these conditions, we are searching for power to get the crew hiking or on the trapeze. Remember that the kicking strap bends the mast and depowers the sails, so it is not required.

Likewise, the Cunningham will bend the mast through compression and ease the upper leech, resulting in less pointing, so leave this off.

Simply use the main and jib sheet to control the leech tension and hence pointing. Just as in light winds, if the boat feels stalled and seems to be slow, try easing the sheet. Jib cars will start to ease forward from the very light winds to exert more tension on the leech of the jib.

As in very light winds, the centreboard will be adjusted for the point of sail and balance will be very important. Trim may be less important, but still check the transom for drag.

Strong Winds

In strong winds the sails develop excessive power and, because you have already exerted your maximum balance by hiking or trapezing fully, it will be necessary to depower. The trick is to sail the boat flat, easing the sails in the gusts and sheeting in for the lulls.

- Tension the kicker to control the leech twist as you play the mainsheet. This is because if the boom rises as you ease the mainsheet, the sail will develop more power which will heel the boat further.
- Jib sheet cars can move aft again, reducing the tension on the leech, increasing the tension on the foot and aiding twist thereby depowering the jib.
- The Cunningham can finally be used, as it will compress and bend the mast, flatten the sail and twist open the leech in the upper part of the sail.

Upwind, balance combined with speed will be a key factor. If the boat slows then the forces (heel) will build very quickly and the boat will simply fall over while going very slowly.

Keep easing sails to maintain some speed through the water, even if this hinders pointing. In moderate gusts you can get away with just easing the mainsail, but in the bigger gusts ease the jib sheet. Otherwise the jib slot will choke as you are playing so much mainsheet.

Once sailing downwind, the forces will be handled by steering – the lower you sail, the less the heeling force on the boat. Trim well back to counteract the forward forces on the rig.

Staying Upright

The wind in the sail and the force created by the daggerboard acts under the boat, creating a heeling force. If this force is too great, the boat may capsize. Keelboats use the weight of a fixed keel to keep them upright, while dinghies and multihulls rely on the weight and position of the crew.

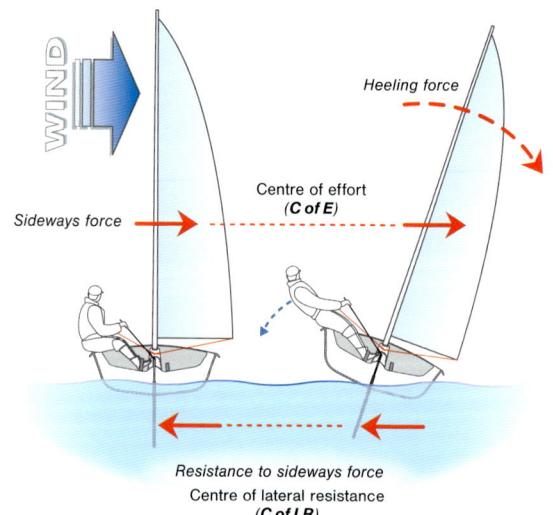

118   RYA Advanced Sailing

On catamarans, try to flatten the sail:

1. Increase downhaul and mainsheet tension and play the traveller.
2. Open the jib slot by moving the jib cars back or out (if you can).

On dinghies:

1. Boat balanced, crew fully hiked.
2. Weight forward but adjusted to allow bow to rise in waves (trim).
3. Centreboard partly raised to ease heeling.
4. Mast raked back to reduce power.
5. Full kicker tension to bend mast and flatten sail.
6. Full Cunningham to flatten sail, twisting top half open and bringing power forward in mainsail.
7. Outhaul tight to depower (looser in waves as you need power).
8. Sail flat to reduce power.
9. Leech tell tales streaming.
10. Luff tell tales just streaming with jib cars further back.

Class Setup

Specific setup makes a big difference and varies from class to class, so consult your class association and rig-tuning guide.

Mast 'rake' is used as a primary means of powering up or depowering most rigs. This can easily be altered by moving the position of the shroud pins.

Tides

As dinghies sail relatively slowly, tide can be a key factor and make a crucial difference to your performance. See pages 47–50 in chapter 3, Day Sailing, for more details. Your strategy will depend upon the strength of the tidal flow.

Look out for headlands, shorelines and the opportunity to escape or use tidal flow to your advantage. Study tide tables and a tidal stream atlas before departure to see how much impact it will have on your sailing in the predicted wind.

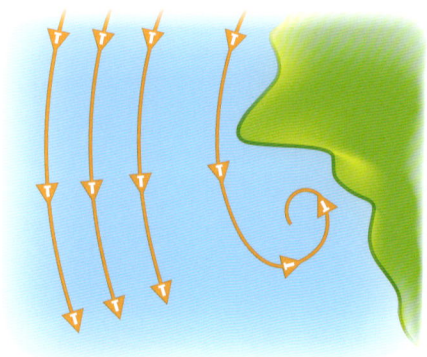

> **TOP TIP**
>
> Look at the race marks and committee boat to see the direction and speed of the tidal stream.

Waves

You will rarely have flat water if sailing on the sea or a large body of inland water. To use the waves, use body movement (balance), steering and trim to harness or cancel the extra force of waves.

When the boat is lifted by a wave it is exposed to stronger, cleaner breeze and is likely to heel.

Sailing upwind, you will generally need to depower the boat as you are raised into the stronger breeze. Steer up the face of the wave and move weight back, and bear away down the back face and move forwards. You may need to ease the mainsail slightly on the top of the wave and pull it back on as you sail down the back. Downwind conditions are more in your favour. Instead of shedding power as the boat is picked up by the wave, encourage the boat to surf down the face.

Trim forward with body weight and pump the jib and mainsheet to promote surfing. Once surfing, continue to trim to the new apparent wind on the sails. Move down the face of the wave, trying to gain as much distance to leeward as possible without falling off the face. If your bow is about to rise into the back of the next wave in front, steer either way to prevent this and trim the sails to suit. Move back to help the bow to rise.

> **TOP TIP**
>
> In waves, always try to sail with the bow pointing slightly down the wave.

Foiling

Hydrofoil vessels have been used on the water for many years. Motorised and sailing craft alike have adopted foils to decrease the level of drag in the water and increase the boat speed and efficiency.

There are several types of foil used in sailing and, historically, dinghies have used a design of foil called 'T-foils'.

Vertical section
Replacing original rudder and daggerboard

Integrated push rod

Moving trim flap

Fixed section

Horizontal foil

Detachable tips

Foiling Boats

There are a variety of boats, including single-handers, double-handers, and multihulls. Some are adaptions through the addition of a foiling kit, while others are dedicated designs.

What is a Foil and How Does it Work?

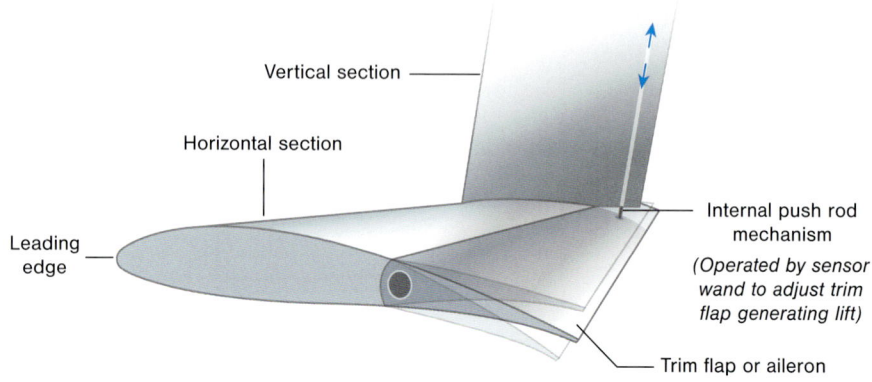

A foil is generally made up of vertical and horizontal foil sections, which replace the traditional rudder and daggerboard.

As the boat speed increases, pressure builds on the foils, and a lifting force is created, similar to an aeroplane wing. This lift brings the boat out of the water, reducing drag and greatly increasing the speed of the boat.

Foil Adjustment

Both the horizontal and vertical foils can be adjusted, each affecting the performance and lift of the boat.

Vertical Foil Adjustment

By adjusting the amount of lift generated, a balance can be found between the two foils, depending on the speed and angle the sailor is looking for.

- Angling the vertical foils towards the front of the boat will increase lift.
- Angling the vertical foils towards the back of the boat will decrease lift.

Horizontal Foil Adjustment

All adjustments increase or decrease the angle of attack on the horizontal foils and therefore affect how much lift the foils are producing.

You can often pre-set the foils before leaving the shore, depending on the boat, and by adjusting both the main and rudder foil the boat's ride height and pitch/trim is affected. It's also often possible to make finer adjustments to the foils while sailing.

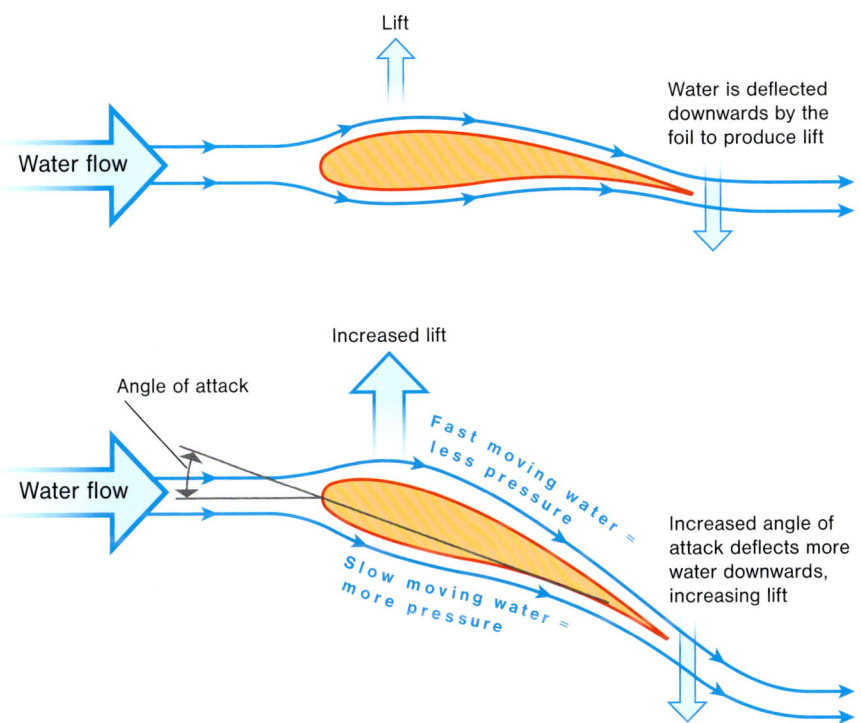

- The main foil can be adjusted to angle the foil or leading edge up or down.
- The rudder-foil angle is often adjusted through a twist-grip tiller, and affects the trim of the boat, bow down or bow up.

Ride Height

Ride height is the amount of vertical lift created through the foil controls, managing the distance the hull flies above the water.

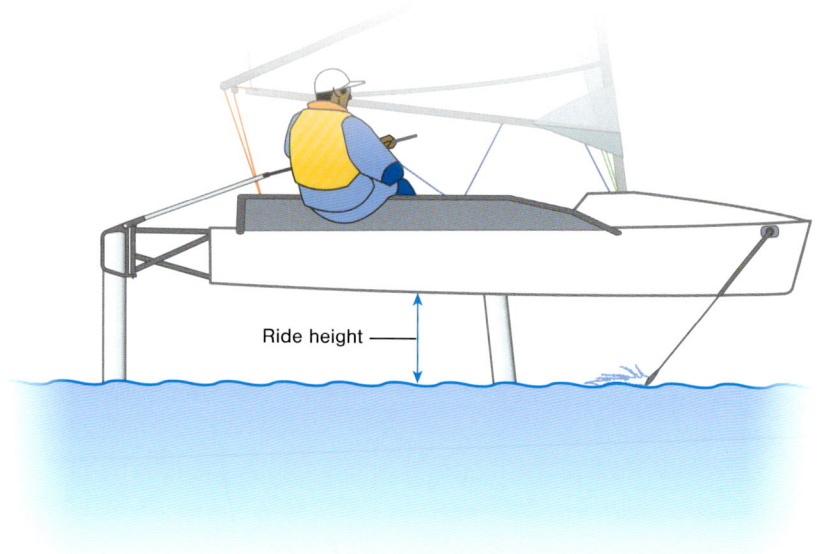

Before leaving the shore, the ride height can be set through adjustment of the main foil lift, which controls how much lift can be created. However, on some boats, fine adjustments to the foils can be made on the water, in-board for the main foil, or through twisting the tiller for the rudder foil.

Without any ride-height control, the boat would simply continue to lift out of the water as speed increases, eventually crashing.

Some foils are designed to control height passively with no moving parts, while on a dinghy the most effective way is with a wand. The wand provides active control of the horizontal foil by moving fore and aft, depending on how high the boat is flying above the surface of the water. The wand controls main-foil trim, automatically adjusting the lift, to provide accurate ride-height control.

The Control Systems

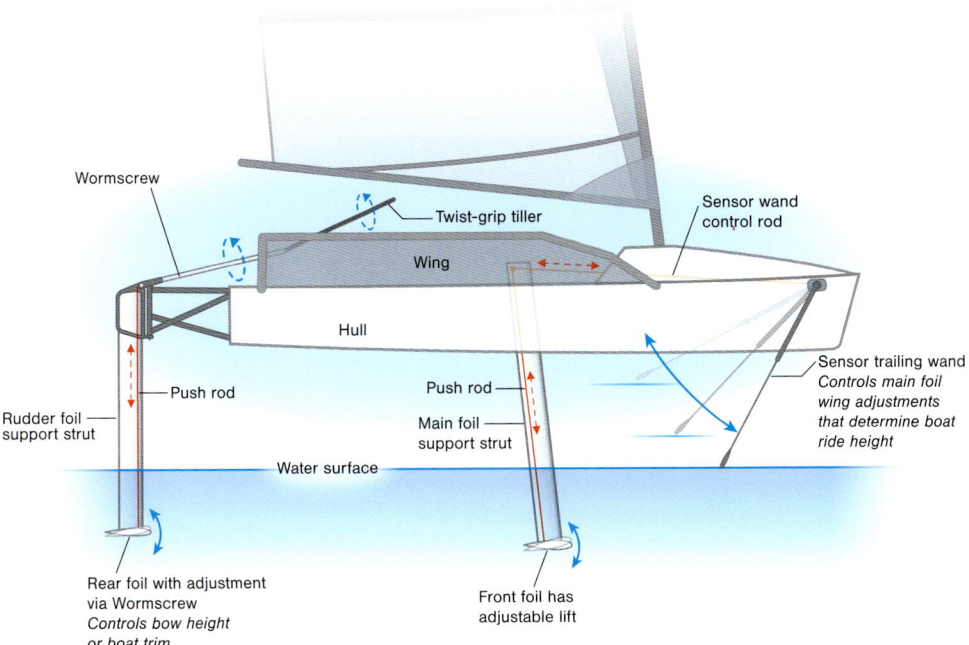

Main Foil:

- The main foil lifts the boat out of the water.

Rudder Foil:

- Controls boat trim and bow height by altering stern lift. This can be controlled on many foiling boats while foiling with a twist-grip tiller.

Wand:

- Fitted to the bow or main foil, the wand controls the lift of the main foil, making ongoing adjustments while sailing to alter a boat's ride height.
- By adjusting the connection from the wand to the main foil, sailors can control the overall ride height by controlling how much lift is created over the foil.

Tiller:

- When a twist-grip tiller is an option, sailors can control the boat trim and bow height while sailing by increasing or decreasing the lift on the rudder horizontal foil.

Leaving and Returning to Shore

Some boats have foils which can be retracted, making launching and recovery relatively easy, whereas others have foils which entail fitting from underneath the boat, requiring you to capsize the boat ashore.

Leaving the shore: As with all boats, it is good practice to carry out 'pre-launch checks' prior to launching, ensuring:

- The foils work and are correctly fitted.
- The wand or trim system is working and correctly fitted.
- The foil attachments are in working order and correctly fitted.
- The launch area (ashore and afloat) is checked and free of obstacles.

For boats with foils inserted from underneath, once you are on the water's edge with the mast across the wind, you can approach the boat from the stern, walk to the foot of the mast, and lift the boat into the water at its balance point. Once you have walked deep enough into the water you can right the boat through the dry-capsize method (avoiding weight on the foils) before sailing away.

Returning to shore: If possible, stop the boat near to a close reach, assisting the depowering of the rig and ease of landing. Return to displacement sailing mode with continuous awareness of water depth, stopping before running aground.

Apparent Wind

Apparent wind is the combination of the 'true wind' and the 'induced wind'.

As a boat's speed increases and it starts to foil, it can go much faster than the true wind speed. This requires the sailor to trim the sails to the apparent wind. For example, if a boat sails on an angle downwind, due to its speed, its sail setting would actually be sheeted in, set to the apparent wind.

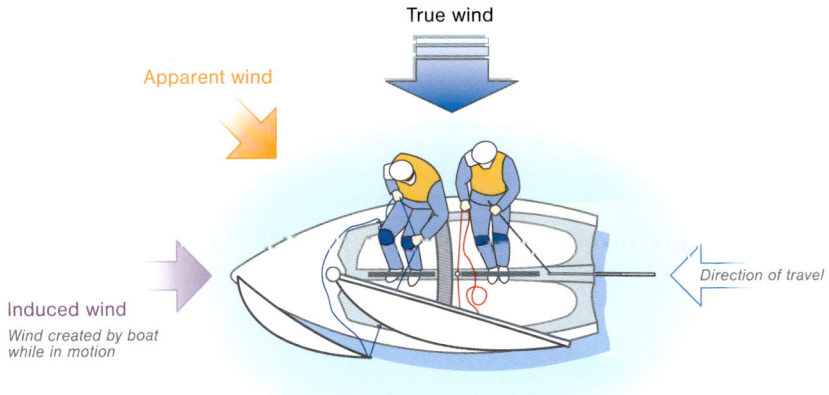

Due to the reduction in drag and the dramatically increased speeds of foiling boats, the need to adjust the sails and boat angle to the apparent wind is more critical than in slower craft.

Flight – Take Off

Once the foils are set up to ensure the boat will fly, the following practical techniques are needed to take off:

- Balance (boat) – Place your weight just behind the mainsheet with the boat heeled to windward.
- Sail setting – Trim the sail to balance the boat with heel to windward.
- Course – Generally, you will need to head on a reach (or close reach) to generate sufficient speed and pressure for take-off. Choosing which reach will depend on how much speed is required by the individual design.

Flight – Sustaining Foiling

With correct main-foil setup, including wand and ride height, and rudder-foil setup, bow height, and boat trim, the following practical techniques are needed for sustained flight:

- Balance (boat) – For best performance, the boat should be heeled slightly to windward. When ready to sail, choose a goal point and adopt a dynamic sailing position, ready to move when the boat begins to gain momentum.
- Sail Setting – Once you have taken off, trim the sail for boat balance, and sheet in, trimming to the apparent wind angle. Continuous trimming to maintain windward heel is needed to keep the boat balanced and on the foils.
- Course – Steer the boat to the desired course, re-trimming as required to maintain windward heel. Keep the boat under the rig, preventing heeling to leeward and capsizing.

Capsize Recovery

To recover from a capsize, the standard dry-capsize method may be used. Be careful not to stand on the foils, and check that they are in full working order before righting the boat.

8 THE RYA NATIONAL SAILING SCHEME

Following the basics of Levels 1 and 2, there is a choice of courses to enable you to pursue whichever part of the sport you wish. All the courses can be taken in a minimum of two days, in keelboats, dinghies or multihulls, or could be clinic based.

THE RYA NATIONAL SAILING SCHEME MODEL

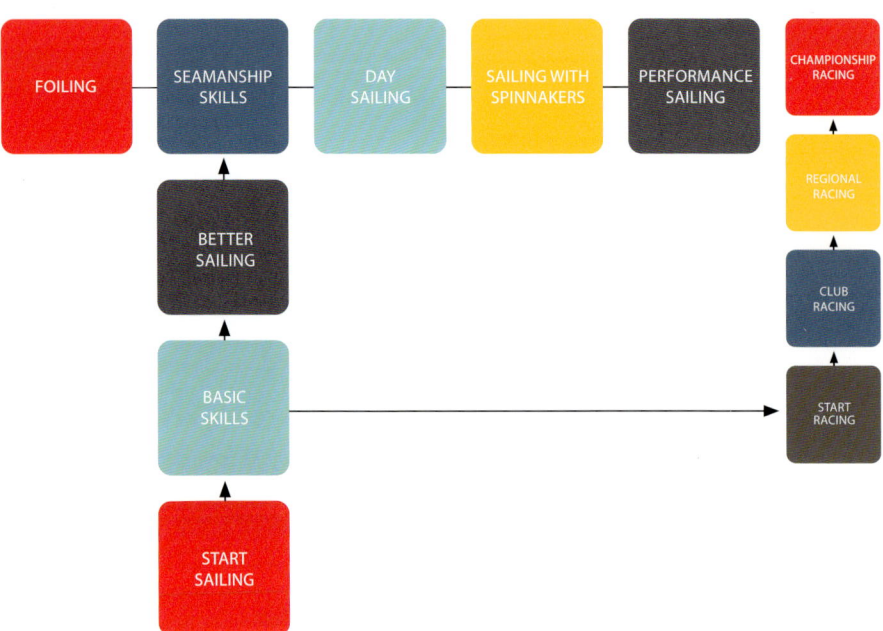

GLOSSARY

Angle of attack	The angle of a wing or foil in relation to the water flowing over it.
Apparent wind	The direction and speed of the wind, affected by course and speed of boat.
Back (verb)	(1) Rotate anti-clockwise, or against the sun.
Backed	(2) A sail filled by the wind in reverse to the normal direction.
Balance	How level the boat is.
Bear away	Turning away from the wind.
Bias	The angle of the start line to the wind if not 90°.
Buoy	A floating mark used for navigation or mooring.
Burgee	A small flag at the top of the mast.
Centreboard	A hinged plate used to resist sideways movement (leeway).
Cleat	A device for securing a rope.
CMG	Course Made Good.
COG	Course over the Ground.
Cunningham	A line for tensioning the leading edge of the sail (downhaul).
Daggerboard	A plate used to resist leeway, inserted vertically and not hinged (see centreboard).
Deviation	Deflection of a compass needle by other magnetic materials.
Displacement	Non-planing dinghy, with speed limited by its hull design.
Downhaul	See Cunningham.
Falls	Rope hanging free after passing through block, e.g. mainsheet falls.
Fully battened	Sails with full width battens, from luff to leech.
Gradient wind	Wind due to weather systems, not local effects.
Gybe (verb)	To turn the boat so that the wind blows from the opposite side, going downwind.
Halyard	Rope or wire used to raise sails and to tension leading edge.
Header	Wind shift taking you further from your upwind objective.
Heeling	Leaning over.
Kicker	Rope or wire used to control twist in the mainsail.

Lay line	Imaginary line along which one can sail to a windward mark without tacking.
Leech	The back edge of the sail.
Leeward	The side of the boat that the wind is blowing away from, i.e. the downwind side.
Leeway	Sideways drift of the boat due to wind pressure.
Lift	Wind shift taking you closer to your upwind objective.
Luff (noun)	The leading edge of the sail.
Luff (verb)	To turn the boat towards the wind.
Mast rake	The angle of the mast to vertical.
Mooring buoy	A buoy used to park a boat.
Neap tides	The period in a month when the tidal range is smallest.
Outhaul	The line used to tension the foot of the sail horizontally.
Planing	Skimming over the surface of the water on a bow wave.
Rocker	The amount of curve in the bottom of a boat.
Sheet	A rope used to control the angle of the sail to wind.
SOG	Speed over the Ground.
Spinnaker	A balloon-shaped sail used downwind.
Spring tides	The period in a month when the tidal range is greatest.
Tack (noun)	The side of the boat opposite the boom, usually the side the wind is coming from, i.e. port tack or starboard tack.
Tack (verb)	Turning the boat so that the wind blows from the opposite side, facing upwind.
Toll talo	Wool or lightweight tape used to detect airflow.
Tidal Range	The difference between high and low water.
Transit	Two fixed objects in line.
Trim	Fore and aft adjustment of weight in the boat.
Variation	The difference in direction between the grid and magnetic north.
Veer (verb)	Rotate clockwise or in the same direction as the sun. See 'Back'.
VMG	Velocity Made Good.
Warp	A rope used for an anchor or mooring.
Waypoint	A chart position put into a GPS memory.
Windward	The side of the boat that the wind is blowing onto, i.e. the upwind side.